NOTARY PUBLIC GUIDEBOOK FOR NORTH CAROLINA

Tenth Edition 2006

NOTARY PUBLIC GUIDEBOOK FOR NORTH CAROLINA

Tenth Edition 2006

Updated and extensively revised by Charles Szypszak

School of Government, UNC Chapel Hill

ESTABLISHED IN 1931, the Institute of Government provides training, advisory, and research services to public officials and others interested in the operation of state and local government in North Carolina. The Institute and the university's Master of Public Administration Program are the core activities of the School of Government at The University of North Carolina at Chapel Hill.

Each year approximately 14,000 public officials and others attend one or more of the more than 200 classes, seminars, and conferences offered by the Institute. Faculty members annually publish up to fifty books, bulletins, and other reference works related to state and local government. Each day that the General Assembly is in session, the Institute's *Daily Bulletin*, available in electronic format, reports on the day's activities for members of the legislature and others who need to follow the course of legislation. An extensive Web site (www.sog.unc.edu) provides access to publications and faculty research, course listings, program and service information, and links to other useful sites related to government.

Operating support for the School of Government's programs and activities comes from many sources, including state appropriations, local government membership dues, private contributions, publication sales, course fees, and service contracts. For more information about the School, the Institute, and the MPA program, visit the Web site or call (919) 966-5381.

Michael R. Smith, DEAN
Thomas H. Thornburg, SENIOR ASSOCIATE DEAN
Ann Cary Simpson, ASSOCIATE DEAN FOR DEVELOPMENT AND COMMUNICATIONS
Bradley G. Volk, ASSOCIATE DEAN FOR FINANCE AND BUSINESS TECHNOLOGY

FACULTY

Gregory S. Allison
Stephen Allred (on leave)
David N. Ammons
A. Fleming Bell, II
Maureen M. Berner
Frayda S. Bluestein
Mark F. Botts
Joan G. Brannon
Mary Maureen Brown
Anita R. Brown-Graham
Shea Riggsbee Denning
James C. Drennan
Richard D. Ducker
Robert L. Farb
Joseph S. Ferrell

Milton S. Heath Jr.
Cheryl Daniels Howell
Joseph E. Hunt
Willow S. Jacobson
Robert P. Joyce
Diane M. Juffras
David M. Lawrence
Donna G. Lewandowski
Janet Mason
Laurie L. Mesibov
Kara Millonzi
Norma Mills
Jill D. Moore
Jonathan Q. Morgan
Ricardo S. Morse

David W. Owens
William C. Rivenbark
John Rubin
John L. Saxon
Jessica Smith
Carl W. Stenberg III
John B. Stephens
Charles A. Szypszak
Vaughn Upshaw
A. John Vogt
Aimee N. Wall
W. Mark C. Weidemaier
Richard B. Whisnant
Gordon P. Whitaker

CONTENTS

PREFACE

This is the tenth edition of the School of Government's *Notary Public Guidebook* for North Carolina. It reflects extensive revisions made to the notary public statutes in 2005 and 2006 by the General Assembly, including a comprehensive overhaul of the Notary Public Act and enactment of the new Electronic Notary Act. The revisions clarify many aspects of notary practice, make many sound practices compulsory, and establish a framework for notarization of electronic records based on standards not yet developed. The changes are so extensive that readers of prior editions should not assume that any previous discussion continues to be reliable. Notaries should consult this edition as if the notary laws were entirely new.

The first edition of this book, by Elmer R. Oettinger and Harry W. McGailliard, was published in 1939; the second edition, by Royal G. Shannonhouse and Willis Clifton Bumgarner, in 1956; the third, by Ann H. Phillips, in 1965; and the fourth, by J. Ritchie Leonard and Patrice Solberg, in 1977. For sixteen years, with the fifth (1984), sixth (1991), seventh (1995), and eighth (2000) editions, Professor William A. Campbell established a legacy of clarity and reliability for which the School of Government and notaries public throughout the state remain indebted. Senior Associate Dean Thomas H. Thornburg maintained this high standard with the ninth edition published in 2004.

Rights of considerable consequence may depend on the correct performance of the notarial function. This book is intended to help notaries learn about the notary office and the performance of notarial duties by combining law, sample forms, and standards of practice into a brief, systematic, and convenient reference work. It also should be of substantial value to registers of deeds, clerks of superior court, and practicing attorneys.

The School of Government wishes to thank North Carolina Secretary of State Elaine F. Marshall and her staff for their valuable assistance in the production of this guidebook. Materials for the discussion of motor vehicle titles were provided by the North Carolina Department of Transportation's Division of Motor Vehicles. I wish to express a personal note of appreciation to Senior Associate Dean Thomas H. Thornburg for his guidance and excellent suggestions and to Charles Moore, Visiting Lecturer at the School, for his support and wise counsel.

CHARLES SZYPSZAK
ASSOCIATE PROFESSOR OF PUBLIC LAW AND GOVERNMENT
Summer 2006

NOTARY PUBLIC GUIDEBOOK FOR NORTH CAROLINA

Tenth Edition 2006

CHAPTER 1

THE OFFICE

1.1 The Notary's Role

The notary public office has long played an important role in commercial affairs. It can be traced back thousands of years to the early Roman Empire. In the seventeenth and eighteenth centuries, as merchants and shippers ventured far from local markets, the notarial function became especially important. This was because commercial agreements entered into in distant places required acknowledgment in a manner that would be respected at home.[1]

Notaries public were part of North Carolina's early legal fabric. In 1777 the North Carolina General Assembly authorized the governor to appoint "from time to time . . . one or more persons, properly qualified, to act as notary or notaries at the different ports in this state."[2] In 1799 the General Assembly authorized the appointment of notaries in every North Carolina county.[3] Today there are more than 168,000 notaries throughout North Carolina.

Although the office of notary public has existed for centuries, its significance is undiminished in modern transactions. Notaries play an important role in preventing fraud and provide a means of validating records of certain actions and agreements. They verify the identity of individuals executing documents that transfer valuable property or establish important legal rights or obligations. By insisting on proper identification and witnessing the signature or other act being notarized, notaries discourage fraud and could provide a means of uncovering attempted identity theft. As improved technology simplifies record creation and duplication, the notary's personal involvement in transactional formalities is an increasingly important human safeguard.

The notary's involvement provides more than a means of confirming identity. By being present when important documents are executed, notaries contribute to a solemn atmosphere that lends weight to the seriousness of the event and deters carelessness. For example, a real estate conveyance is often the most substantial financial transaction of a person's life. A signature on a deed or mortgage is a significant event that deserves careful attention. Notaries play a vital role in this process. Similarly, by being part of the formalities involved in the execution of wills, notaries help individuals who are recording their wishes for their families' future appreciate the importance of their actions.

The official record the notary provides may be a puzzle piece that will be essential to those who later need to assess a record's legitimacy many years after the event with which the document is associated occurs. In real estate transactions, for example, purchasers may be relying on the legitimacy of instruments in the public record that contain signatures and notary acknowledgments completed generations earlier. In addition, the record of a notary's acts can help reconstruct events long after the participants are gone, memories have faded, or recollections have taken on conflicting versions. For example, a will may determine the disposition of a lifetime's earnings, but its authenticity is unlikely to be examined until after the person who signed it is deceased.

The notarial act may be perceived as an unnecessarily cumbersome and formalistic exercise. But the notarial observance of formality and the fine details of careful notarial practice

---

1. For a more detailed history of notaries, see Lawrence G. Greene, LAW OF NOTARIES PUBLIC 1 (Legal Almanac Series No. 14, 2d rev. ed. 1967, ed. Dusan J. Djonovich and Robert Sperry); Edward M. John, JOHN'S AMERICAN NOTARY AND COMMISSIONER OF DEEDS MANUAL § 2 (6th ed. 1951, by Frederick H. Campbell). See 58 AM. JUR. 2d *Notaries Public* §§ 1–71 (2002) for additional background about notaries.

2. Laws of N.C., ch. 8, § 15 (1777).

3. Laws of N.C., ch. 15 (1799).

could be decisive factors in validating an important transaction or in unraveling a fraudulent scheme. North Carolina laws for notary qualification and education and the rules directing how notarial acts must be performed and documented are intended to ensure that the notarial process sustains its credibility. North Carolina citizens depend on notaries to know and follow the law and rules for the performance of official notarial acts.

In all cases, including those occasions when the rules do not provide specific direction, notaries may be guided by Thomas Jefferson's advice:

> Whenever you are to do a thing, though it can never be known but to yourself, ask yourself how you would act were all the world looking at you, and act accordingly.[4]

1.2 Applicable Law

All fifty states have notaries, and the laws governing notarial practices are becoming increasingly uniform. Nonetheless, the manner of appointment, the tenure of office, and notarial powers and duties may vary from state to state. A North Carolina notary should never assume that he or she may do what a notary in another state may do; the powers and duties of a North Carolina notary are determined by North Carolina law. The laws governing the notary office and notarial acts and powers are set out in Chapter 10B of the General Statutes, entitled Notaries. Chapter 10B is reproduced in Appendix 1 in the version current as of the date of publication of this guidebook.

1.3 Process for Becoming a Notary

A person must meet certain qualifications to become a notary in North Carolina. To obtain a commission, qualified applicants must first complete a course of education, pass an examination, submit an acceptable application to the North Carolina Department of the Secretary of State (hereinafter the Department), and comply with certain other requirements. The Department issues notary commissions and regulates notary conduct.

1.3.1 Qualifications

The Notary Act sets out the qualifications for becoming a notary. The statutes limit eligibility to persons eighteen years old or older; who reside legally in the United States and can speak, read, and write English; who possess a high school diploma or equivalent; and who reside or have a regular place of work or business in North Carolina. The statute defines a *regular place of work or business* as "[a] location, office or other workspace, where an individual regularly spends all or part of the individual's work time."[5] An applicant who resides in North Carolina is commissioned in the county of residence. An applicant who is a nonresident is commissioned in the county in North Carolina where he or she is regularly employed or maintains a place of business.[6]

---

4. Thomas Jefferson to Peter Carr, 19 August 1785. Thomas Jefferson Letters 1743–1826, Electronic Text Center, University of Virginia Library, etext.virginia.edu/etcbin/toccer-new2?id=JefLett.sgm&images=images/modeng&data=/texts/english/modeng/parsed&tag=public&part=32&division=div1 (accessed August 24, 2006).

5. N.C. GEN. STAT. § 10B-3(20) (hereinafter G.S.).

6. G.S. 10B-5(c).

Under the dual-officeholding provisions of the North Carolina Constitution, a person serving as a notary is expressly authorized to hold concurrently another elective or appointive state or federal office.[7]

The North Carolina Constitution and the North Carolina General Statutes identify circumstances that disqualify a person from becoming a notary. A person may not become a notary if he or she has been (1) convicted of a felony under North Carolina or federal law, (2) convicted in another state of a felony if the crime would also be a felony had it been committed in North Carolina, (3) convicted of corruption or malpractice in any office, or (4) removed from any office by impeachment and not restored to the rights of citizenship as prescribed by law.[8] Additional statutory grounds for denial of a notary commission are as follows:

- Conviction of or plea of admission or nolo contendere to a felony or any crime involving dishonesty or moral turpitude (*moral turpitude* is "[c]onduct contrary to expected standards of honesty, morality, or integrity"[9]). The Department will not consider issuing a commission to an applicant until ten years after release from a sentence of prison, probation, or parole for conviction of these offenses, whichever is later.[10]
- Finding or admission of liability in a civil lawsuit based on the applicant's deceit.[11]
- Revocation, suspension, restriction, or denial of a notarial commission or professional license by North Carolina or another state or nation. The Department will not consider issuing a commission to an applicant until five years after the completion of all conditions of any disciplinary order relating to such matters.[12]
- Finding of official misconduct, regardless of whether disciplinary action resulted.[13]
- Knowing use of false or misleading advertising in which the applicant, as a notary, represented that the applicant had powers, duties, rights, or privileges he or she did not legally possess.[14]
- Finding by a state bar or court that the applicant has engaged in the unauthorized practice of law.[15]

1.3.2 Notary Course and Examination

Before initial appointment as a notary, applicants must complete a Department-approved course on notarial laws, procedures, and ethics.[16] (Attorneys licensed to practice in North

---

7. N.C. CONST. art. VI, § 9(2).

8. N.C. CONST. art. VI, § 8. The state constitution also disqualifies from public office those who "deny the being of Almighty God," but this disqualification is not enforced because it clearly violates the First Amendment of the United States Constitution. Torcasco v. Watkins, 367 U.S. 488 (1961); 41 N.C. Att'y Gen. Rep. 727 (1972).

9. G.S. 10B-3(9).

10. G.S. 10B-5(d)(2).

11. G.S. 10B-5(d)(3).

12. G.S. 10B-5(d)(4).

13. G.S. 10B-5(d)(5).

14. G.S. 10B-5(d)(6).

15. G.S. 10B-5(d)(7).

16. G.S. 10B-8.

Carolina are exempt from this requirement.)[17] Approved courses are offered by all North Carolina community colleges and other institutions as approved by the Department and include a minimum of six hours of classroom instruction.[18] The nonattorney applicant must apply for his or her commission within three months of successfully completing the course,[19] and the application must include the signature of the instructor and the date on which the course was successfully completed. (Applications also must include the signature of an elected official, as described in section 1.3.4 below.)

A nonattorney applicant for an initial commission or recommission also must pass a written examination approved by the Department and administered under its direction. The examination is given at the end of the notary course. To pass the exam, the applicant must answer at least 80 percent of the questions correctly.[20] (Attorneys licensed to practice in North Carolina are not required to take the exam.)[21]

1.3.3 Required Manual

Before being commissioned, all applicants (including attorneys) must purchase and retain for reference the most recent manual approved by the Department.[22] The currently approved manual may be purchased from the School of Government's Publications Office at 919-966-4119 or online at php.unc.edu/sogcart.

1.3.4 Commission Application

All persons applying for a notary commission must submit an application to the North Carolina Department of the Secretary of State. The application can be obtained from any register of deeds office or from the Department at the following address: Notary Public Section, Department of the Secretary of State, P.O. Box 29626, Raleigh, North Carolina 27626-0626. Applications may also be obtained online at the Department's Web site, www.sosnc.com or www.secretary.state.nc.us/notary.

The application for a notary commission contains a statement of personal qualification. This statement includes the applicant's full legal name (no nicknames). The applicant also must provide the following information:

- Date of birth
- Mailing and street address and telephone number
- County of residence
- Name, mailing and street address, and telephone number of employer
- Last four digits of Social Security number
- Personal and business e-mail addresses
- A declaration of United States citizenship or proof of legal residency in this country
- A declaration of ability to speak, read, and write English
- A complete listing of any issuances, denials, revocations, suspensions, restrictions, and resignations of a notarial commission, professional license, or public office involving the applicant in any state or nation

17. G.S. 10B-8.
18. G.S. 10B-8(a).
19. G.S. 10B-8(a).
20. G.S. 10B-8.
21. G.S. 10B-8(a).
22. G.S. 10B-5(b)(7).

- A complete listing of any criminal convictions, including any pleas of admission or nolo contendere, in any state or nation
- A complete listing of any civil findings or admissions of fault or liability regarding the applicant's activities as a notary in any state or nation[23]

The application requires a recommendation from a North Carolina elected official unless the applicant will be taking the oaths from the register of deeds of a county where more than 15,000 active notaries public are on record on January 1 of the year in which the application is filed.[24] As of the publication of this edition, the exception applies only in Wake County. A register of deeds or a clerk of court who is the applicant's notary course instructor may sign the application at the course's conclusion both as the instructor and as the recommending elected official. Instructors may not, however, notarize applications for any of their students.

The application must be signed in pen and ink by the applicant and acknowledged before a person authorized to administer oaths.[25]

The seriousness of the application is reflected by a requirement that the following declaration, given under oath or affirmation, be made with the application for a notary public commission:

Declaration of Applicant

I, _____ (name of applicant), solemnly swear or affirm under penalty of perjury that the information in this application is true, complete, and correct; that I understand the official duties and responsibilities of a notary public in this State, as described in the statutes; and that I will perform to the best of my ability all notarial acts in accordance with the law.

_____
Signature of Applicant[26]

The applicant must return the completed application with the recommendation and a check or money order for the statutory fee of $50, payable to the Secretary of State of North Carolina. This nonrefundable fee is required for the issuance of the commission.[27]

1.3.5 Review of Commission Application

The director of the Notary Public Section in the Department of the Secretary of State attempts to verify the information provided in selected applications. Constitutional and statutory grounds for disqualification are discussed in section 1.3.1 above. An application for a commission or recommission also may be denied if the application is incomplete or contains a material misstatement or omission of fact.[28]

---

23. G.S. 10B-7(a).
24. G.S. 10B-5(b)(9).
25. G.S. 10B-5(b)(8).
26. G.S. 10B-12.
27. G.S. 10B-13.
28. G.S. 10B-5(d)(1).

1.3.6 Oaths of Office

Unless an application is incomplete or inaccurate or an investigation reveals that an applicant is disqualified from serving as a notary, the Department's policy is to issue a commission upon receiving the completed application showing that the applicant has taken the training course and passed the qualifying examination. If the application is approved, the Department notifies the appointee about the procedure for taking the oaths. The Department sends the newly appointed notary's commission, along with an oath notification letter, to the register of deeds of the county where the oaths are to be administered.[29] The appointee must then appear before the register of deeds in the county of commission within forty-five days of the commission's effective date, which is shown on the oath notification letter.[30] Notaries take the following oath prescribed for all public officials:

> I, _____, do solemnly and sincerely swear that I will support the Constitution of the United States; that I will be faithful and bear true allegiance to the State of North Carolina, and to the constitutional powers and authorities which are or may be established for the government thereof; and that I will endeavor to support, maintain and defend the Constitution of said State, not inconsistent with the Constitution of the United States, to the best of my knowledge and ability, so help me God.[31]

Persons with conscientious scruples against taking an oath in the manner described above may substitute the word "affirm" for the word "swear" and may delete the words "so help me God."[32]

Notaries also take the following notary oath of office:

> I, _____, do swear (or affirm) that I will well and truly execute the duties of the office of notary public according to the best of my skill and ability, according to law; so help me, God.[33]

The notary must pay a $10 fee to the register of deeds who administered the oaths.[34]

The oaths must be taken promptly. If the appointee does not appear before the register of deeds within forty-five days of the commission's effective date, the register is to return the commission to the Department. The applicant must then reapply for a commission, including submitting a new application and fee.[35]

After taking the oaths, the notary signs his or her name exactly as it appears on the commission in the "Record of Notaries Public" maintained by the register of deeds. If the Department ever revokes the commission, the revocation date also will be entered in the record book. After the notary signs the book, the register of deeds delivers the commission to the notary. The register then completes the certificate of qualification and returns it to the Department. The Department permits the "Record of Notaries Public" to be maintained in electronic format as long as the notaries' signatures may be viewed and printed.[36]

---

29. G.S. 10B-10(a).
30. G.S. 10B-10(b).
31. G.S. 11-7.
32. G.S. 11-4.
33. G.S. 11-11.
34. G.S. 161-10(a)(17).
35. G.S. 10B-10(e).
36. G.S. 10B-10(c).

A person issued a commission may not perform any of the duties of the office until he or she appears before the register of deeds of the county where commissioned and takes the oaths of office.[37] Performing a notarial act before a person takes the oaths of office is a Class 1 misdemeanor criminal offense and grounds for restriction, suspension, or revocation of the commission.[38] Notarial acts are invalid if performed before a required oath is taken.[39]

1.4 Term

A commission is not effective until the applicant takes the oaths of office.[40] A notary's commission is valid for five years unless the commission is revoked or resigned.[41] A notary's commission expiration date is printed on the commission certificate; the commission expires at midnight on that date.

1.5 Recommissions

Notary public commissions are not renewed; each subsequent commission is a new appointment, and with each new appointment a notary must requalify for a commission by completing the application process successfully and retaking the oaths of office. There is no limit to the number of successive appointments a notary may serve.

A notary may apply for recommissioning no earlier than ten weeks before expiration of a current commission.[42] The notary who submits an application for recommissioning follows the same procedure as for initial commissioning, including submitting the completed application form and paying the $50 application fee, with three exceptions.

- The notary course need not have been taken and a high school diploma is not required.[43]
- The publicly elected official and notary instructor signatures are not required.[44]
- The examination can be completed online. The Department offers the online examination for recommissioning on its Web site at www.sosnc.com. The examination need not be taken for recommissioning by attorneys nor by notaries who have been continuously commissioned since July 10, 1991, and who have not been disciplined by the Department.[45]

An application for recommissioning is also offered online but is limited to those who take the online examination. Attorneys, who are not required to take the examination, should mail their applications and the $50 application fee to the Department.

A notary who applies for recommissioning after commission expiration but within one year of the expiration follows the same procedure as if applying before commission expi-

---

37. G.S. 10B-9.
38. G.S. 10B-60(a); G.S. 10B-60(b)(3).
39. G.S. 10B-9.
40. G.S. 10B-9.
41. G.S. 10B-9.
42. G.S. 10B-11(a).
43. G.S. 10B-11(b)(2).
44. G.S. 10B-11(b)(1); G.S. 10B-11(b)(2).
45. G.S. 10B-11(b)(3).

ration.[46] Although the statutes authorize it to do so,[47] the Department does not require these applicants to retake the notary course if they pass the examination. A former notary who applies for recommissioning more than one year after commission expiration must follow the procedure for an initial appointment.

Notaries must not perform official acts after a commission has expired and before the oaths are taken for another term. Performing a notarial act after a commission has expired is a Class 1 misdemeanor criminal offense.[48]

1.6 Change of Name or Location

A notary who changes his or her name, residence, business address, mailing address, or telephone number is required to notify the Department, within forty-five days of the change, by fax, e-mail, or certified mail, return receipt requested, providing both the old and new information.[49] A notary whose name has changed may continue to use the former name in performing notarial acts until he or she completes the steps required for using the new name. These steps are as follows: (1) the notary must notify the Department of the name change and receive confirmation that the notice has been received; (2) the notary must obtain a new official seal with the new name; and (3) within forty-five days after the effective date of the change, the notary must retake the oaths of office before the register of deeds in the county of commissioning.[50] The notary should not begin using the new name in notarial acts until these steps have been completed.

A notary who changes county of residence may continue to notarize without obtaining a new seal, but upon recommissioning the notary must obtain a new seal and take the oaths before the register of deeds of the new county.[51]

1.7 Electronic Notary Registration

North Carolina adopted the Electronic Notary Act in the 2005 legislative session.[52] The law validates electronic notarial acts made in connection with electronic records. The precise methods of performing these acts are to be governed by standards to be adopted by the Department.[53]

A person must first be a duly commissioned notary to be qualified to become an electronic notary.[54] A notary must register the capability to notarize electronically with the Department and pay a $50 fee for the registration.[55]

Electronic notaries must have completed an additional three hours of instruction and have passed an electronic notary examination approved by the Department.[56]

---

46. G.S. 10B-11(c).
47. G.S. 10B-11(c).
48. G.S. 10B-60(b)(2).
49. G.S. 10B-50; G.S. 10B-51.
50. G.S. 10B-51(b).
51. G.S. 10B-52.
52. G.S. 10B-100 to G.S. 10B-146.
53. G.S. 10B-125(b).
54. G.S. 10B-105(a)(1).
55. G.S. 10B-106(a) to G.S. 10B-106(c); G.S. 10B-108.
56. G.S. 10B-107.

1.8 Commission Termination and Enforcement

A notary's commission can be resigned voluntarily or it can be terminated or restricted under certain circumstances.

1.8.1 Resignation

A notary who resigns must send a signed notice of resignation to the Department by fax, e-mail, or certified mail, return receipt requested, indicating the effective date of resignation.[57] Notaries who cease to maintain a residence or regular place of work or business in North Carolina, or whose inability to be present in the state makes them permanently unable to perform their notarial duties, are required to resign.[58] The notary who resigns must deliver the notary's seal to the Department by certified mail, return receipt requested, within forty-five days of the effective date of resignation.[59]

1.8.2 Secretary of State Enforcement and Penalties

The Department may issue a warning to a notary or restrict, suspend, or revoke a notary's commission for a violation of the notary laws and on any ground for which a commission could have been denied.[60] This would include, for example, having omitted a material fact from an application for commission; engaging in false or misleading advertisement about notarial authority; or, as is most often the case, taking an acknowledgment, verification, proof, or performing an oath or affirmation without the principal being present.

The Department's staff of investigators and enforcement personnel examines every complaint concerning notarial misconduct. If the investigation establishes that there has been a violation, the Department may seek criminal prosecution or civil penalties such as notary commission revocation or suspension. If the Department institutes disciplinary action, the notary has sixty days to make a written appeal. This appeal must be filed with the North Carolina Office of Administrative Hearings and the General Counsel of the Secretary of State. Once a petition has been filed with the Office of Administrative Hearings, the petitioner will be notified how to proceed.

When a commission is revoked or suspended, both the notary and the register of deeds in the county in which the notary is commissioned receive a copy of the suspension or revocation order. The order becomes effective two days from the date of the letter. As described in section 1.9 below, the performance of notarial acts after revocation or suspension is a criminal offense.[61]

A notary's resignation or commission expiration does not terminate or preclude an investigation by the Department.[62] The Department may continue to pursue the investigation to a conclusion and the results may become a matter of public record regardless of whether the finding would have been grounds for disciplinary action.[63]

---

57. G.S. 10B-54(a).
58. G.S. 10B-54(b).
59. G.S. 10B-55(a).
60. G.S. 10B-60(a).
61. G.S. 10B-60(b).
62. G.S. 10B-60(h).
63. G.S. 10B-60(h).

1.9 Criminal Offenses

Notaries public are entrusted with responsibilities to the public. Consequently, notaries must adhere to the legal requirements for performing notarial acts and avoid engaging in fraudulent or deceptive acts or practices. Anyone who performs notarial acts without proper authority violates the law. Such violations could result in criminal prosecution and penalties, including incarceration. The Notary Act categorizes the following actions by anyone as Class 1 misdemeanors:

- Publicly representing oneself as a notary without being commissioned[64]
- Performing a notarial act after one's commission has expired or been suspended or restricted[65]
- Performing a notarial act before taking the oaths of office[66]

The following actions by a notary are Class 1 misdemeanors:

- Taking an acknowledgment or administering an oath or affirmation without the principal appearing in person before the notary[67]
- Taking a verification or proof of a subscribing witness without the subscribing witness appearing in person before the notary[68]
- Taking an acknowledgment or administering an oath or affirmation without personal knowledge or satisfactory evidence of the principal's identity[69]
- Taking a verification or proof without personal knowledge or satisfactory evidence of the subscribing witness's identity[70]

The following actions by a notary are Class I felonies:

- Taking an acknowledgment, verification, or proof, or administering an oath or affirmation, if the notary knows it is false or fraudulent[71]
- Taking an acknowledgment or administering an oath or affirmation without the principal appearing in person before the notary if the notary does so with the intent to commit fraud[72]
- Taking a verification or proof without the subscribing witness appearing in person before the notary if the notary does so with the intent to commit fraud[73]

The following actions by anyone constitute Class I felonies:

- Performing notarial acts in North Carolina knowing he or she is not commissioned under the North Carolina Notary Act[74]

---

64. G.S. 10B-60(b)(1).
65. G.S. 10B-60(b)(2).
66. G.S. 10B-60(b)(3).
67. G.S. 10B-60(c)(1).
68. G.S. 10B-60(c)(2).
69. G.S. 10B-60(c)(3).
70. G.S. 10B-60(c)(4).
71. G.S. 10B-60(d)(1).
72. G.S. 10B-60(d)(2).
73. G.S. 10B-60(d)(3).
74. G.S. 10B-60(e).

- Obtaining, using, concealing, defacing, or destroying a notarial seal or notary records without authority[75]
- Wrongfully obtaining, using, concealing, defacing, or destroying the certificate, disk, coding, card, program, software, file, or hardware enabling an electronic notary to affix an official electronic signature[76]

The following action by anyone constitutes a Class G felony:

- Knowingly creating, manufacturing, or distributing software for the purpose of allowing a person to act as an electronic notary without being commissioned and registered in accordance with the North Carolina Electronic Notary Act[77]

1.10 Summary of Procedural Requirements for Changes in the Status of a Notary Public

Change	Procedural requirements	Fee
Initial commissioning	• Successfully complete 6-hour notary public course and pass instructor-administered exam, within 3 months before application to Department of the Secretary of State (except N.C. attorneys) • Submit application to the Department • Receive oath notification letter from the Department • Take oaths of office at register of deeds in county of commission within 45 days • Possess current Department-approved manual	$50
Recommissioning before commission expiration	• Pass examination within 3 months before commission expiration (except N.C. attorneys and notaries continuously commissioned since July 10, 1991, without discipline) (online exam available on Department's Web site, www.sosnc.com) • Submit new application to the Department before, but no earlier than 10 weeks prior to, commission expiration • Receive oath notification letter from the Department • Take oaths of office at register of deeds in county of commission within 45 days	$50

---

75. G.S. 10B-60(f).
76. G.S. 10B-146(b).
77. G.S. 10B-146(a).

Change	Procedural requirements	Fee
Recommissioning after commission expiration but within 1 year	• Pass examination (except N.C. attorneys and notaries continuously commissioned since July 10, 1991, without discipline) (online exam available on Department's Web site, www.sosnc.com) • Submit new application to the Department • Receive oath notification letter from the Department • Take oaths of office at register of deeds in county of commission within 45 days*	$50
Name change	• Submit signed notice of change to the Department within 45 days after name change • Receive oath notification letter from the Department • Obtain new seal • Return old seal to the Department by certified mail, return receipt requested • Retake oaths of office at register of deeds in county of commission within 45 days	None
Address change within same county	• Submit signed notice of change to the Department within 45 days after address change	None
Name and county change	• Submit new application to the Department within 45 days after name change • Receive oath notification letter from the Department • Obtain new seal • Return old seal to the Department by certified mail, return receipt requested • Take oaths of office at register of deeds in county of commission within 45 days	$50
County change only	• Upon recommissioning, comply with recommissioning requirements • Upon recommissioning, obtain new seal • Return old seal to the Department by certified mail, return receipt requested	$50
Resignation/relocation outside of N.C.	• Submit resignation letter to the Department within 45 days • Return seal to the Department by certified mail, return receipt requested	None
Death of notary	• Estate notifies the Department in writing • Estate delivers seal to the Department as soon as reasonably practicable but before estate closes	None

*Notaries should not perform official acts after a commission has expired and before taking the oaths of office for the new commission. Doing so is a Class 1 misdemeanor. See section 1.9 above.

CHAPTER 2
POWERS AND LIMITATIONS

2.1 Powers

North Carolina law states: "A notary is a public officer of the State of North Carolina and shall act in full and strict compliance" with the Notary Public Act.[1] A public official has only the powers granted by law and must strictly adhere to the limits of that authority. Notaries must not use their offices or seals in ways not prescribed in the Notary Act, even if such powers are commonly assumed. For example, a North Carolina notary may not certify a true copy of a document; the statutes give this authority to particular other officials.

A duly commissioned North Carolina notary is authorized by law to perform four types of notarial acts:

- Acknowledgments
- Oaths and affirmations
- Verifications and proofs[2]

---

1. N.C. GEN. STAT. §10B-3(13) (hereinafter G.S.).
2. G.S. 10B-20(a).

Each involves the notary's observance of another's actions and the creation of a certificate to record the event. In each case the notary must be concerned both with the nature of the action observed and the manner in which the record of that action is made. *Acknowledgments* are records a notary makes on a document indicating that the notary witnessed a properly identified person execute a document or confirm having signed it. An *oath* or *affirmation* is a vow of truthfulness made before a notary. With an oath the individual whose action is being notarized invokes a deity or uses any form of the word "swear"; with an affirmation the individual makes a vow based on personal honor without invoking a deity or using the word "swear." *Verifications* and *proofs* are certifications made under oath or affirmation to a notary that a person witnessed someone else execute a record or acknowledge a signature, or that the person recognized a signature.

The specific requirements for each of these acts are described in Chapter 3, "Notarial Procedures." The certificates used to record these acts are described in Chapter 4, "Certificates."

2.2 Limitations and Requirements

As described above, notaries may perform only the acts authorized by law and may perform them only according to the law. Notaries are specifically constrained by a number of limitations and requirements.

2.2.1 Jurisdiction

A North Carolina notary may act within any county of the state of North Carolina,[3] regardless of the location of the subject matter of the transaction or of the residence of the persons who are signing the instrument or for whose benefit the instrument is made. When a notary acts outside his or her home county, the county name in the official seal will not match the county name in the certificate heading. For example, if a Davidson County notary certifies a document in Rowan County, the certification will begin with "North Carolina, Rowan County" and the notary's seal image will show that the notary is commissioned in Davidson County, not in Rowan County.

North Carolina does not recognize acts of out-of-state notaries performed within this state.[4] For example, an attestation made by a South Carolina notary while visiting North Carolina is invalid, and so, too, is an official act made by a North Carolina notary while in another state.

A North Carolina notary may perform within this state a notarial function regarding a transaction to be made in another state, if the notarial function is authorized by the other state's law and is to be performed for some purpose that is proper within that state. In addition, acts of a notary of another state properly performed within his or her home state are fully recognized in North Carolina insofar as they are authorized by the home state's law, North Carolina law, or federal law.[5] For example, an attestation made by a South Carolina notary within South Carolina according to South Carolina law is valid in this state.

Laws governing particular instruments may have additional requirements in order for the notary's actions to have the force intended by the drafter of the instrument. For example, if a notary of another state takes the proof or acknowledgment for an instrument to

---

3. G.S. 10B-9.
4. *See* County Sav. Bank v. Tolbert, 192 N.C. 126, 133 S.E. 558 (1926).
5. G.S. 10B-20(f).

be recorded with a North Carolina register of deeds but does not affix the notary's seal or stamp and commission expiration date thereon, the county official before whom the notary qualified for office must certify that the notary was an acting notary at the time the certificate was made and that the notary's signature is genuine. This officer's certificate must be under seal and must accompany the notary's certification of the instrument.[6]

2.2.2 Unauthorized Practice of Law

The General Statutes prohibit notaries from "assist[ing] another person in drafting, completing, selecting, or understanding a record or transaction requiring a notarial act" [7] because a notary who is not a licensed attorney may not practice law.[8] The practice of law includes, but is not limited to, the following, whether rendered with or without compensation: preparing or helping to prepare deeds, deeds of trust, mortgages, wills, or similar documents; abstracting or advising on titles to real or personal property; and giving opinions about someone's legal rights.[9] However, a notary as a private citizen may prepare deeds or other instruments for a transaction to which he or she is a party[10] as well as notarial certificates to be executed by him- or herself as a notary. A notary may not notarize his or her own signature.

Although the "practice of law" encompasses a wide range of activities, a notary should be attentive to two particular areas in which confusion is likely to occur—real estate transactions and matters involving immigration. The practice of law issue as it relates to real estate transactions is of special concern to paralegals and others who work for attorneys of title companies. The North Carolina State Bar, which has statutory authority to investigate charges of unauthorized practice of law and to bring legal action to enjoin it,[11] has issued formal ethics opinions concluding that a person not licensed as an attorney may not "handle" a residential real estate closing because these transactions involve elements of practicing law. However, a person who is not a licensed attorney (regardless of whether the person is working under an attorney's supervision) may present and identify the documents necessary to complete a real estate closing, direct the parties where to sign the documents, ensure that the parties have properly executed the documents, and receive and disburse closing funds.[12] An attorney may delegate these ministerial tasks to someone whom he or she is supervising.[13] Or, a person having no relationship with the attorney and who is not licensed to practice law may perform these limited administrative duties.[14] Anyone who is not an attorney should avoid performing any services that may appear to involve providing legal interpretation or giving legal advice. Specifically, the State Bar's opinion is that engaging in any of the following activities in connection with a residential real estate transaction constitutes the unauthorized practice of law:

---

6. G.S. 47-2.2.

7. G.S. 10B-20(k).

8. G.S. 84-4.

9. G.S. 84-2.1.

10. *See* State v. Pledger, 257 N.C. 634, 127 S.E.2d 337 (1962).

11. G.S. 84-37.

12. N.C. State Bar, Formal Ethics Opinion 2002-9 and Authorized Practice Advisory Opinion 2002-1, both issued on January 24, 2003. These opinions are available at the State Bar's Web site at www.ncbar.com/index.asp.

13. N.C. State Bar, Formal Ethics Opinion 2002-9.

14. N.C. State Bar, Authorized Practice Advisory Opinion 2002-1.

- Providing abstracts or opinions on title to real property
- Explaining the legal status of title to real property or the legal effect of any-thing found in the chain of title or of any item reported as an exception in a title insurance commitment
- Giving advice about rights and responsibilities of parties—whether unsolicited or in response to a party's question or to resolve a dispute between the par-ties—under circumstances requiring legal judgment or having implications for the parties' legal rights or obligations
- Instructing a party to the transaction about alternative ways for taking title to the property or the legal consequences of taking title in a particular manner
- Drafting legal documents for a party to the transaction or assisting a party in the completion of a legal document, or assisting the party in selecting a form legal document among several forms having different legal implications[15]

The Notary Act specifically prohibits a notary from "claim[ing] to have powers, qualifi-cations, rights, or privileges that the office of notary does not provide, including the power to counsel on immigration matters." [16] In the context of immigration, issues involving the practice of law arise essentially because of an unfortunate linguistic coincidence between English and Spanish. In Latin American countries, a *notario publico* is a state-appointed, private legal professional who has duties that are in important respects similar to those of a lawyer in the United States. Because of the similarity between the terms *notario publico* and "notary public," concern exists that Latino immigrants may seek legal advice from notaries public, mistakenly believing that they are receiving advice from legal profession-als. To avoid the inadvertent compromise of such a person's legal situation, as well as outright fraud, many states, including North Carolina, have placed restrictions on nota-ries' interactions with the immigrant community. Restrictions on advertising in languages other than English originate from concerns about the unauthorized practice of law and are discussed in section 2.2.7 below.

2.2.3 Photographs
A notary is not authorized to certify, notarize, or authenticate a photograph. A notary may notarize an affidavit regarding and attached to a photograph.[17]

2.2.4 Marriage Ceremony
A notary may not perform a marriage ceremony unless he or she is also an ordained or authorized minister, magistrate, or has other authority recognized by law.[18]

2.2.5 Judicial Functions
While many notarial duties are quasi-judicial, a notary's powers are limited to those specifically granted by statute. Unless he or she is also a judicial officer, the notary may not issue warrants, summonses, or subpoenas; preside over civil or criminal proceedings; or issue judgments, decrees, or orders.

---

15. N.C. State Bar, Formal Ethics Opinion 2002-9.
16. G.S. 10B-20(n).
17. G.S. 10B-23(b).
18. G.S. 51-1.

2.2.6 Electronic Records

A notary having a regular commission may perform notarial acts only in connection with a record that is "inscribed on a tangible medium and called a traditional or paper record."[19] A notarization in connection with an electronic record may only be performed by a notary who (1) has registered the capability to notarize electronically with the Department of the Secretary of State,[20] (2) has completed an additional course of instruction and examination for electronic notaries,[21] (3) has paid a registration fee for electronic notary status,[22] and (4) complies with all other requirements for performing an electronic notarial act.[23] Electronic notaries are described in greater detail in section 1.7 above.

2.2.7 Advertisements

North Carolina law provides that nonattorney notaries who advertise notarial services in a language other than English must give conspicuous notice with the advertisement (either in writing or orally, depending on the medium of the advertisement), in English and the appropriate language, stating, as provided by statute: "I am not an attorney licensed to practice law in the state of North Carolina, and I may not give legal advice or accept fees for legal advice."[24] Notaries required to post this notice must also prominently post at their places of business a fee schedule in English and the non-English language in which they advertise.[25] In addition, notaries who are not licensed attorneys may not represent themselves as "immigration consultants" (unless they are recognized as such by the U.S. Board of Immigration Appeals).[26]

2.2.8 Testimonials

A notary is prohibited from using "the official notary title or seal in a manner intended to endorse, promote, denounce, or oppose any product, service, contest, candidate, or other offering."[27] This restriction does not prohibit a notary from notarizing a document intended to accomplish these goals.

2.3 Fees

The maximum fees that a notary may charge are as follows:

- For acknowledgments, jurats, verifications or proofs: $5 per principal signature
- For oaths or affirmations without a signature: $5 per person (except for oaths or affirmations administered to credible witnesses to vouch for the identity of a principal or subscribing witness)[28]

---

19. G.S. 10B-3(19).
20. G.S. 10B-106(a).
21. G.S. 10B-107.
22. G.S. 10B-108.
23. G.S. 10B-100 to G.S. 10B-146.
24. G.S. 10B-20(i).
25. G.S. 10B-20(l).
26. G.S. 10B-20(j).
27. G.S. 10B-24.
28. G.S. 10B-31.

For performing an electronic notarial act, a notary may charge $10 per signature for an acknowledgment, jurat, verification or proof, or oath or affirmation.

Notaries who charge must conspicuously display a fee schedule in English (no less than ten-point type) in their places of business or present it outside their places of business.[29]

---

29. G.S. 10B-32.

CHAPTER 3

NOTARIAL PROCEDURES

3.1 Performance of the Notarial Act

When performing an authorized notarial act, the notary must adhere to laws governing how the act should be conducted and how a record of the event is to be made. Each of these procedures involves certain prescribed actions, which are described in this chapter. Chapter 4, "Certificates," describes the records that must be made in association with various notarial acts. The only notarial act that a notary may perform without completing a certificate is an oath or affirmation,[1] but most oaths and affirmations concern records on which a certificate is needed.

The notary law uses the term *principal* to refer to an individual, other than a credible witness, whose identity and due execution of a record are certified or who is making an oath or affirmation. A *credible witness* is someone who confirms a signer's identity.[2] A *subscribing witness* is a person who confirms having witnessed someone else sign a record or acknowledge having signed it.[3]

In an *acknowledgment*, the notary must ensure that the following occur:

- A principal appears in person at a single time and place before the notary and presents a record.
- The principal is personally known to the notary or identified by the notary through satisfactory evidence as defined by law.
- The principal signs the record in the notary's presence or indicates to the notary that the signature is the principal's.[4]

In a *verification* or *proof*, the notary must ensure that the following occur:

- An individual appears in person at a single time and place before the notary and presents a record already executed by a principal.
- The individual is personally known to the notary or identified by the notary through satisfactory evidence as defined by law.
- The individual certifies to the notary under oath or affirmation that he or she is not a party to or a beneficiary of the transaction.
- The individual makes an oath or affirmation to the notary that the subscribing witness witnessed the principal either sign the record or acknowledge having signed it, or the individual recognized either the principal's signature, or the signature of a subscribing witness, as genuine.[5]

The following are required for an *oath* involving a record:

- A principal appears in person at a single time and place before the notary.
- The principal is personally known to the notary or identified by the notary through satisfactory evidence as defined by law.
- The principal either signs the record before the notary or states to the notary that the principal voluntarily signed the record for the purposes stated therein.

---

1. N.C. GEN. STAT. § 10B-23(a) (hereinafter G.S.).
2. G.S. 10B-3(5); G.S. 10B-3(18).
3. G.S. 10B-3(26).
4. G.S. 10B-3(1); G.S. 10B-40(a1)(1).
5. G.S. 10B-3(28); G.S. 10B-40(a1)(4).

- The principal makes a vow of truthfulness about the matters stated in the record, on penalty of perjury, while invoking a deity or using any form of the word "swear."[6]

An *affirmation* of a record has the same legal effect as an oath and requires the same conditions, but the vow is "based on personal honor and [made] without invoking a deity or using any form of the word 'swear.'"[7]

In some circumstances notaries may take an oath or affirmation that does not involve any type of record, as described in section 3.6 below. In these cases the vow involves the truth of a commitment, such as in an oath of office.

3.2 Notarization Requirements

The law specifies certain requirements for any notarization.

3.2.1 Personal Appearance

The principal or subscribing witnesses must appear personally before the notary during the notarial act.[8] *Personal appearance* means that the individual and "notary are in close physical proximity to one another so that they may freely see and communicate with one another and exchange records back and forth during the notarization process."[9] Lack of personal appearance by the principal or subscribing witness is one of the most common notary act violations. The law does not allow exceptions to this requirement based on the notary's familiarity with the individual or the individual's course of business. A notary violates the law if the notary accepts confirmation of a signature by phone or by an instruction left by the signatory. Any attempted acknowledgment by telephone, telegraph, mail, or any other means that does not bring the acknowledger physically before the notary is invalid.[10] Taking an acknowledgment or oath or affirmation without the principal personally appearing before the notary is a Class 1 misdemeanor[11] and a Class I felony if the notary does so with the intent to commit fraud.[12] In addition, it is unethical for an attorney to file a document for public record when the attorney has personal knowledge that the acknowledger did not physically appear before the certifying notary.[13]

The personal appearance requirement may seem inconvenient to those who regularly rely on notaries to acknowledge numerous instruments in the ordinary course of business. But personal appearance is an essential part of the lawfully performed notarial act, providing the notary with eyewitness confirmation of the action to which the notary is officially attesting and lending weight to the seriousness of the event. Insisting that the principal or subscribing witness sign before the notary need not be viewed as an indication of mistrust of a familiar person; it is a precaution against someone else using that relationship to commit fraud.

---

6. G.S. 10B-3(14); G.S. 10B-40(a1)(2), (3).
7. G.S. 10B-3(2).
8. G.S. 10B-20(c)(1).
9. G.S. 10B-3(16).
10. *See* Southern State Bank v. Sumner, 187 N.C. 762, 122 S.E. 848 (1924).
11. G.S. 10B-60(c)(1).
12. G.S. 10B-60(d)(2), (3).
13. N.C. State Bar, Ethical Opinion 720 (1970).

3.2.2 Identification

For each of the authorized notarial acts, any principal or subscribing witness must be personally known to the notary or be identified through satisfactory evidence.[14]

The statute defines *personal knowledge of identity* as "[f]amiliarity with an individual resulting from interactions with that individual over a period of time sufficient to eliminate every reasonable doubt that the individual has the identity claimed."[15] Personal knowledge must therefore be based on a history of familiarity.

Satisfactory evidence is either sufficient documentary evidence or confirmation by a credible witness. Identification usually is by means of the required documentary evidence. Satisfactory documentary evidence of identity must consist of "[a]t least one current document issued by a federal, state, or federal or state-recognized tribal government agency bearing the photographic image of the individual's face and either the signature or a physical description of the individual."[16] Satisfactory documentary evidence from a government jurisdiction is not limited to that issued by United States federal or state authorities; it could consist of an official government identification card issued in another country, provided that the card is currently valid and includes the individual's photographic image and his or her signature or physical description. The notary should examine the information on the presented identification for a match to the individual who presents it and for apparent legitimacy. The notary should not rely on identity cards that show signs of tampering or alteration.

The second form of satisfactory evidence is an "oath or affirmation of one credible witness who personally knows the individual seeking to be identified."[17] The law defines *credible witness* as "[a]n individual who is personally known to the notary" whom "[t]he notary believes . . . to be honest and reliable for the purpose of confirming to the notary the identity of another individual" and whom "[t]he notary believes . . . is not a party to or a beneficiary of the transaction."[18] These definitions make clear, first, that the witness must be already personally known to the notary—the notary cannot rely on documentary identification for a witness who is identifying the subject of the notarial act. Secondly, the definitions also clarify that the notary must believe that the witness is not a party to or a beneficiary of the transaction to which the instrument being executed pertains (such as being the grantee of a deed or the beneficiary of a will). As stated above, the credible witness must make the identification under oath.

3.2.3 Signature of Principal or Subscribing Witness

For an acknowledgment or oath or affirmation, the principal signs the record. For a verification or proof, the subscribing witness signs the record on which a signature already appears. A signature can be the customary script version of a name or a mark made or adopted by the signer with the intention of authenticating the document.[19] If a signature is made by mark, the mark must be affixed in the notary's presence, and the notary must write the following below the mark: "Mark affixed by *(name of signer by mark)* in presence of undersigned notary."[20]

---

14. G.S. 10B-20(c)(2); G.S. 10B-20(c)(2a).
15. G.S. 10B-3(17).
16. G.S. 10B-3(22)(a).
17. G.S. 10B-3(22)(b).
18. G.S. 10B-3(5).
19. State v. Watts, 289 N.C. 445, 222 S.E.2d 389 (1976).
20. G.S. 10B-20(d).

If a principal is physically unable to sign or make a mark on a record presented to the notary, the principal may designate another person to sign on the principal's behalf.[21] The designated person must be a "disinterested party"[22]—someone who will not personally benefit from the transaction being recorded. The act must be witnessed by at least two other witnesses as well, who also must be unaffected by the record. The principal directs the designated person to sign in the principal's name, in front of the two witnesses and the notary. Both witnesses also sign their own names to the record near the principal's signature. The notary writes below the principal's signature: "Signature affixed by designee in the presence of (*names and addresses of principal and witnesses*)."[23]

When an instrument is executed for another person by an attorney-in-fact under a power of attorney, the attorney-in-fact may sign the instrument either in the principal's name by the named attorney-in-fact ("John Smith by Robert Jones, attorney-in-fact"), or in the attorney-in-fact's name for the named principal ("Robert Jones, as attorney-in-fact for John Smith").[24] In any event the instrument should indicate the capacity in which the document was signed. It is misleading and incorrect for the attorney-in-fact merely to sign the principal's name and for the notary to indicate in the certificate that the principal signed.

3.3 Disqualifying Circumstances

Chapter 2, "Powers and Limitations," describes the limits of a notary's authority, including jurisdictional boundaries. The following circumstances disqualify a notary from performing a notarial act.

3.3.1 Conflict of Interest

A notary is disqualified from performing a notarial act if the notary is a signer of the document or a party to or a beneficiary of it. This disqualification does not apply to a notary whose involvement with the record is as a trustee in a deed of trust. The disqualification also does not apply to a notary whose only involvement is as an attorney to a party to the document, or whose only involvement with the record is as a person named in it as a drafter or to whom it is to be returned after recording.[25] Additionally, a notary is disqualified from acting as a notary if he or she will receive directly from a transaction connected with the notarial act any commission, fee, advantage, right, title, interest, cash, property, or other consideration in excess of the notarization fees allowed by the Notary Act, which are described in section 2.3.[26] Fees or other consideration for services rendered by a lawyer, real estate broker or salesperson, motor vehicle dealer, or banker are excluded for purposes of determining this disqualification.[27] Essentially, if a notary will receive anything of value from the transaction other than the notary fees (except for the services listed above), the notary is disqualified. Many laws have validated the acts of notaries who were also interested parties in transactions for which they performed notarial acts,[28] but most of this curative legislation applies only to past transactions. The hope of such future curative legislation is not a sound basis for a notary to become involved in questionable practices.

---

21. G.S. 10B-20(e).
22. G.S. 10B-20(e).
23. G.S. 10B-20(e).
24. G.S. 47-43.1.
25. G.S. 10B-20(c)(5).
26. G.S. 10B-20(c)(6).
27. G.S. 10B-20(c)(6).
28. G.S. 47-62 to G.S. 47-64; G.S. 47-92 to G.S. 47-95; G.S. 47-100.

3.3.2 Principal or Subscribing Witness Capacity

By signing a certificate for an acknowledgment or the administration of an oath or affirmation, the notary is certifying, whether stated or not, that the person whose signature was notarized did not appear in the notary's judgment to be incompetent, lacking in understanding of the nature and consequences of the related transaction, or acting involuntarily or under duress or undue influence.[29] A disqualifying circumstance might arise, for example, if a person whose acknowledgment is being taken is elderly and ill and apparently unaware of what is occurring, but someone is directing him or her to sign the instrument.[30]

3.3.3 Known Falsehood

A notary may not execute a notarial certificate containing information the notary knows or believes to be false.[31]

3.3.4 Language Other Than English

A North Carolina notary may execute a notarial certificate only if it is in English.[32] The notary may execute a certificate in English for a document written in another language if the document contains a translation of the certificate into the foreign language. In this case the notary should execute only the certificate that appears in English.[33]A notary may not perform a notarial act if the notary has a compelling doubt about whether the individual knows the consequences of the related transaction, as described in section 3.3.2 above. This prohibition could be implicated if a notary is asked to take the acknowledgment of an individual signing an instrument written in a language the notary knows the individual does not understand.

3.4 Order of Multiple Notarial Acts

When an instrument has been signed by more than one person, the acknowledgments need not be made in the same order as the signatures, nor must the certificates of acknowledgment appear in any particular order. Furthermore, an instrument executed by several different persons may be acknowledged by each of them before the same notary or before different notaries at different times and in different places. The certificates must reflect the correct information in each case.

3.5 Attestation Requirements

"Attestation" refers to the notary's completion of evidence of the notarial act. The evidence includes the notary's official seal and signature, the notary's commission expiration date, and a description of the notarial act in the form of a certificate. Chapter 4 describes

---

29. G.S. 10B-40(a2)(2).
30. *See, e.g.,* Griffin v. Bancom, 74 N.C. App. 282, 286, 328 S.E.2d 38, 41 (N.C. App.), *rev. denied,* 314 N.C. 315, 332 S.E.2d 481 (1985).
31. G.S. 10B-22(a).
32. G.S. 10B-22(b).
33. G.S. 10B-22(b).

the forms to be used for various certificates. This section discusses the four other requirements for an attestation:

- The notary's signature, which must be exactly as shown on the notary's commission[34]
- The legible appearance of the notary's name, from the notary's typed or printed name near the signature or elsewhere in the certificate or on the seal[35]
- The clear and legible appearance of the notary's stamp or seal[36]
- A statement of the date the notary's commission expires either on the seal or elsewhere in the certificate[37]

Although numerous statutes validate past notarial certifications from which seals were omitted,[38] notaries should not rely on potential future statutes to correct their errors.

The following are simple examples of correct and incorrect correlation between instances of the notary's name in attestation components.

Correct:

Commission Name: John Allen Smith
Official Signature: *John Allen Smith*

Incorrect Signature:

Commission Name: John Allen Smith
Signature: *John A. Smith*

Correct:

Commission Name: John A. Smith
Official Signature: *John A. Smith*

Incorrect Name on Seal:

Commission Name: John Allen Smith
Official Signature: *John Allen Smith*

John A. Smith
Notary Public
Orange County, NC

---

34. G.S. 10B-20(b)(1).
35. G.S. 10B-20(b)(2).
36. G.S. 10B-20(b)(3).
37. G.S. 10B-20(b)(4).
38. G.S. 47-53, -53.1, -102, and -103.

3.5.1 Notary's Official Signature

Every attestation, whether for an acknowledgment, oath or affirmation, or verification or proof, must include the notary's signature in ink (except as may be authorized by regulation for electronic notaries) written exactly as it appears on the notary's commission.[39] Thus the name in the seal and the signature must always match. Problems most commonly arise with middle initials and with name changes related to marriage or divorce. Notaries must be consistent with the use of middle initials or full middle names as shown on the commission and the seal. A notary whose name changes may not use the new name in a notarial act until he or she takes the oaths for the new commission reflecting the new name (see section 1.6 of this guidebook). Until that time, the notary may continue to use the former name in performing notarial acts.[40]

3.5.2 Official Seal

The notarial seal symbolizes the state power with which the notary has been entrusted. The presence of the seal on a written document raises a presumption that the document was attested in the manner required by law by a notary.[41]

A North Carolina notary may use either a seal that makes an impression or a stamp that uses ink, provided the image is clear and legible. In this book, unless otherwise specified the word "seal" is used to refer to both types. The shape of the seal may be rectangular or circular. If rectangular, the seal may not be more than 1 inch high and 2½ inches long. If circular, the seal must be at least 1½ inches and no more than 2 inches in diameter.[42] (These dimensional requirements do not apply to seals for notaries whose currently effective commisions were issued before October 1, 2006.)[43] Either shape must have a border that is visible when impressed or stamped.[44] The seal must include the name of the notary *exactly* as it appears on the commission, the county of commission including the word "County" or the abbreviation "Co.," the words "North Carolina" or the abbreviation "NC," and the words "Notary Public."[45] The law permits but does not require a notary's commission expiration date to be included, either permanently imprinted or typed or handwritten in space allocated for that purpose.[46] So that the device may be used for more than one term, the Department of the Secretary of State advises against including the commission expiration date on the seal or stamp.

The image of the seal must be placed near and on the same page as the notary's official signature and certificate.[47] This placement will prevent page substitutions after the notarial act. The seal must not be affixed until after the notarial act is performed in each instance.[48] The notary must ensure that a seal by impression will be reproducible. When using a stamp that leaves ink, the notary should be careful not to place it where it will obscure any of the document's text or the certificate's contents.

The notary must safeguard the seal against misuse. The notary must keep it in a secure location and may not allow anyone else to possess it.[49] The notary remains responsible

39. G.S. 10B-20(b)(1); G.S. 10B-35.
40. G.S. 10B-51(b).
41. *See* State v. Knight, 169 N.C. 333, 344, 85 S.E. 418, 424 (1915).
42. G.S. 10B-37(c).
43. G.S. 10B-37(c)
44. G.S. 10B-37(c).
45. G.S. 10B-37(b).
46. G.S. 10B-37(d).
47. G.S. 10B-36(b); G.S. 10B-37(a).
48. G.S. 10B-36(b).
49. G.S. 10B-36(a).

for the seal even if he or she changes employment and may not surrender the seal to an employer upon employment termination.[50] Within ten days of discovering that a seal is stolen or lost, the notary must give written notice of that fact, signed in the notary's official name, to the Department and to the register of deeds of the county in which commissioned.[51] In the case of theft or vandalism, the notary must also notify the appropriate law enforcement agency, likely the sheriff of the county in which commissioned.[52] Seals must be sent to the Department by certified mail within forty-five days after a notary's commission has expired or has been resigned or terminated, except that someone whose commission has expired need not forward the seal if he or she intends to apply for recommissioning and is recommissioned within three months.[53] The estate of a deceased notary should forward the seal to the Department as soon as practicable and before the estate is closed.[54] The Department destroys returned seals.

3.5.3 Notary's Typed or Printed Name
Every notarial act must be attested by the legible appearance of the notary's name, typed or printed near the notary's signature, or in the certificate or seal.[55] Common notarial practice is to print the name immediately beneath the notary's signature line. Reciting the notary's name in the certificate associated with the signature will meet this attestation requirement.

3.5.4 Commission Expiration Date
The notary must indicate the date the notary's commission expires on every attestation.[56] As discussed above, the commission expiration date may be included in the seal, but it is not required to be depicted in this way. If the expiration date is not in the seal, it must be separately stated near the notary's signature. It customarily appears beneath the notary's typed or printed name. Although an erroneous depiction of an expiration date will not invalidate the legal sufficiency of an act by a commissioned notary, notaries should take care to avoid the problems that could arise as a result of such a mistake.[57]

3.6 Oaths and Affirmations

Whenever the notarial certificate contains the words "sworn to" or "duly sworn," the notary must administer an oath to the person whose acknowledgment or proof is being taken. In this guidebook, unless specified otherwise, the word "oath" should be understood to include "affirmation." An affirmation is legally equivalent to an oath but is based on personal honor and does not invoke a deity or use any form of the word "swear."[58]

Under North Carolina law, a notary public may administer any oath, including an oath of office, except when the law requires that another official administer the particular

---

50. G.S. 10B-36(a).
51. G.S. 10B-36(c).
52. G.S. 10B-36(c).
53. G.S. 10B-36(d); G.S. 10B-55. Section 10B-36(d) requires that the seal be delivered to the secretary "[a]s soon as is reasonably practicable," and section 10B-55 sets a limit of forty-five days after resignation or revocation to return the seal.
54. G.S. 10B-55(c).
55. G.S. 10B-20(b)(2).
56. G.S. 10B-20(b)(4).
57. G.S. 10B-67.
58. G.S. 10B-3(2).

oath.[59] For example, a notary may not administer the oath of office to another notary, because a statute specifically provides that notaries must take this oath before a register of deeds.[60] Whenever the law prescribes an oath without specifying the officer before whom it must be taken, a notary may administer the oath. Under federal law, a North Carolina notary acting within North Carolina may administer any oath authorized or required by the laws of the United States,[61] including oaths of office for all federal offices.[62] In addition to this general authorization, notaries are specifically authorized to take oaths of office for national bank directors[63] and oaths with respect to adverse claims of mining rights.[64]

The statute prescribing the oath to be administered provides that the person administering the oath "shall (except in the case in this Chapter excepted) require the party to be sworn to lay his hand upon the Holy Scriptures, in token of his engagement to speak the truth and in further token that, if he should swerve from the truth, he may be justly deprived of all the blessings of that holy book and made liable to that vengeance which he has imprecated on his own head."[65] The words "Holy Scriptures" can be interpreted as referring specifically to the Christian Bible as the only book on which the oath taker's hand is to be placed. If this interpretation is correct, then the statutes do not expressly provide for someone to give an oath by placing a hand on another book considered sacred. Individuals who do not wish to place their hands on the Bible would have two alternatives: giving an oath with "uplifted hand"[66] or giving an affirmation,[67] as described below. However, interpreting the law as specifying the Bible as the only acceptable religious text for an oath makes the statute susceptible to challenge as violating the establishment clause of the First Amendment of the United States Constitution.[68] In another context, the North Carolina Supreme Court recognized the validity of an oath based on another book considered sacred by the oath taker.[69] The statute can be construed consistent with this principle by interpreting the phrase "Holy Scriptures" more broadly to include all books sacred to various religions, which for Christians would be the New Testament or the Bible, for Jews the Torah or the Old Testament, for Muslims the Koran, for Hindus the Bhagavad-Gita, and so forth.[70]

---

59. G.S. 10B-20(a)(2); G.S. 11-7.1(a)(3).
60. G.S. 10B-10(b).
61. 5 U.S.C. § 2903(c)(2).
62. 5 U.S.C. § 2903(a).
63. 12 U.S.C. § 73.
64. 30 U.S.C. § 31.
65. G.S. 11-2.
66. The "oath with uplifted hand" requires an oath taker to stand with his or her right hand "lifted up toward heaven." The oath taker would thus be unable to place his or her right hand on a text considered sacred. G.S. 11-3.
67. In an affirmation, the oath taker does not use the word "swear" or the words "so help me God." The statute does not prohibit placing a hand on a book or document, nor would there be any sound objection if the oath taker did so intending to sanctify or validate the promise being made.
68. See McCreary County v. American Civil Liberties Union of Kentucky, 125 S. Ct. 2722, 2733 (2005) (discussing the constitutional prohibition against favoring a particular religion); Cantwell v. Connecticut, 310 U.S. 296, 303 (1940) (establishment clause applies to states by incorporation of the Fourteenth Amendment).
69. In Shaw v. Moore, 49 N.C. 28 (1856), the North Carolina Supreme Court held that Jews may swear their oath on the Old Testament. The court rejected a more narrow view of the oath requirement and said: "We think it indecent to suppose that the Legislature intended in an indirect and covert manner to alter a well-settled and unquestioned rule of law, and, in despite of the progress of the age, to throw the country back upon the illiberal rule which was supposed to be law in the time of bigotry." Shaw, 49 N.C. at 30.
70. Prior to 1985 the statute for administration of oaths required that the oath taker's hand be placed "upon

The statutes allow an oath taker having conscientious scruples against taking a book oath to stand with

> right hand lifted up toward heaven, in token of his solemn appeal to the Supreme God, and also in token that if he should swerve from the truth he would draw down the vengeance of heaven upon his head, and shall intro-duce the intended oath with these words, namely: "I, [*name of oath taker*], do appeal to God, as a witness of the truth and the avenger of falsehood, as I shall answer the same at the great day of judgment, when the secrets of all hearts shall be known (etc. as the words of the oath may be)."[71]

Instead of taking an oath invoking a deity or using a sacred book, an oath taker may choose to make an affirmation. A person who makes an affirmation rather than an oath should say "affirm" rather than "swear" and should omit the words "so help me God."[72] The person making an affirmation is not required to place his or her hand on any book or document.

Although a statement may be reduced to writing in a notary's presence when it is the sub-ject of an oath or affirmation, it is usually already in writing when brought before the notary. When taking an oath about a written statement, a notary may use the following form:

> Do you swear that the statements contained in this writing are the truth, by your own knowledge or by your information and belief, so help you, God?

A similar affirmation would be as follows:

> Do you affirm, on your personal honor, that the statements contained in this writing are the truth, by your own knowledge or by your information and belief?

After receiving an unqualified affirmative response, the notary may then complete a cer-tificate in the form described in Chapter 4, "Certificates."

3.7 Authentication

Other countries sometimes require documents to be authenticated by a state authority, who in North Carolina is the Secretary of State. The authentication provides the state government's confirmation of the notary's capacity. For example, documents for adoption by North Carolina residents of a child who is a citizen of another country likely must be authenticated by the Department to be recognized in the other country. Notaries should take special care in handling such documents. Delays in authentication occurring because certificates are not in proper form can cause problems for involved parties.

Once a document is authenticated, the Secretary of State signs and issues a certificate of authentication, which bears the state or the secretary's seal, and places it on or appends

---

the Holy Evangelists of Almighty God." N.C. Code § 3309 (1943). In 1985 the oath statutes were revised. Among other things, the phrase "Holy Scriptures" replaced "Holy Evangelists of Almighty God," and the provision for affirmation was added. 1985 N.C. Sess. Laws ch. 756. The change to "Holy Scriptures" can be interpreted as including texts, other than the New Testament or the Bible, that are considered sacred.

71. G.S. 11-3.
72. G.S. 11-4.

it to the document.[73] In international law this certificate is sometimes called an "apostille." When authenticating a document, the Department compares the official's seal and signature on the document to a specimen of the official's seal and signature on file. If such information is not on file, the Department may rely on further authentication by another official for whom the Department does have such information.[74]

Only a document with an original seal and signature may be authenticated; a facsimile, photostat, photographic, or other reproduction of a signature or seal is unacceptable.[75] The acknowledgment must be in English or be accompanied by a certified or notarized translation into English.[76] All dates must be in chronological order on certifications for authentication.[77] Whenever a copy of an authentication is used, it must include a statement, made in a sworn affidavit, that it is a true and accurate copy.[78] The Department may by rule impose additional requirements relating to authentications.[79]

3.8 Notary Journal

Some states require notaries to keep a journal of their official acts. North Carolina law does not presently mandate journals. The Department may adopt a rule requiring electronic notaries to keep journals, but the rule cannot take effect before June 1, 2007.[80]

Notaries should nonetheless consider the benefits, both to themselves and to those who rely on them, of keeping a journal. A journal could prove to be invaluable for reconstructing the events related to a notarial act if the act's validity is later challenged. Memories, especially those about the details of one of many similar events, fade over time, and a journal can become an important historic source. A journal also can confirm a notary's adherence to statutory requirements and good practices. Finally, a journal can be a kind of checklist for notaries, reminding them about each step they must take with every notarial act. Even the most experienced notary can use reminders about careful practices.

A journal should be permanently bound with sequentially numbered pages and entries made without blank spaces, to prevent removal or insertion of pages or entries. An electronic version would have the same safeguards. Most laws requiring journals specify that the following entries be included:[81]

- Date and brief description of each instrument notarized
- Date of notarization
- Type of notarial act (for example, an acknowledgment or verification)
- Location at which the notarial act was performed
- Name and address of each principal and subscribing witness
- How the principal or subscribing witness was identified (description—not specific identification numbers) (including names and addresses of any credible witnesses)
- Fees received by the notary

---

73. G.S. 66-270; G.S. 66-272.
74. G.S. 66-272.
75. G.S. 66-274(b)(3).
76. G.S. 66-273(3).
77. G.S. 66-272(2).
78. G.S. 66-273(4).
79. G.S. 66-273(5).
80. G.S. 10B-126(e).
81. *See, e.g.,* CAL. GOV'T CODE § 8206(a)(1) (2005); Model Notary Act § 7-1 (National Notary Ass'n 2002), www.nationalnotary.org/resources/index.cfm?text=actionModel (accessed August 24, 2006).

If a notary is involved in an act that is not completed due to, for example, fail[...] ject to provide sufficient identification or some other disqualification, the no[...] record the date, names, and circumstances of the incomplete act in the journa[...]

3.9 Some Basic Dos and Don'ts

Some Basic Dos and Don'ts for Notaries	
Do:	**Don't:**
Sign the certificate in the exact name that appears on your commission and seal	Sign your name so that it appears not to match the name on your commission and seal
Insist that the principal personally appear before you at the time of the notarization	Take someone's confirmation of a signature by telephone, telegraph, mail, or an instruction left by a signatory
Place your seal image near your signature	Place your seal image on a different page than your signature
Insist on the required identification if you do not personally know the subject	Rely on the identification of an unknown subject by another unknown person
Keep track of your commission expiration date	Perform a notarial act after your commission expires
Keep sole control of your notary seal	Loan or give your seal to anyone else
Ensure that your embossed seal or stamp image is reproducible by ordinary means	Use a seal or stamp that creates an image too light to be seen when the document is copied
Ensure that the information in your certificate matches the notarial act you are performing	Use a preprinted certificate the contents of which you do not verify upon notarization
Ensure that the certificate is appropriate and complete	If you are not an attorney, give advice about what the contents of the document will legally accomplish
Cross out blank spaces in certificates except when a blank is specifically allowed by law	Use preprinted certificates with blank spaces left empty other than those specifically allowed by law to remain blank
Insist that the subject of an oath or affirmation actually make the vow	Complete a certificate involving an oath or affirmation without requiring the subject to make the oath or affirmation
Report a name change to the Department, obtain a new seal, and retake the oaths	Sign using a new name that does not match your seal
Include the principal's name in the certificate	Sign and seal a document without a complete certificate

CHAPTER 4

CERTIFICATES

4.1 General Requirements

In 2005 and 2006 the Notary Act was substantially revised and it now provides simplified general purpose certificate forms that are consistent with the laws and practices of most other states. Although various special-purpose certificate forms can be found in other statutes such as those pertaining to real estate instruments, estate planning, and corporate conveyances, the revised and simplified Notary Act forms are now sufficient for notarial acts performed in North Carolina and may be used in circumstances in which neither law nor custom requires that special information be included in the certificate. The forms described in the other statutes have not been repealed, however, and may continue to be used.[1] This chapter describes and depicts both the Notary Act forms as well as the other statutory forms.

Many instruments presented to a notary have blank certificate forms already attached. Determining whether the certificate has the desired legal effect is the responsibility of the parties and their attorneys. The notary's duty is to ensure that the recitals of the certificate are accurate. The Notary Act requires that a notary cross out or mark through all blank lines or spaces in certificates.[2] The statute makes an exception only for blank lines or spaces in a notarial certificate for a signature by an attorney-in-fact for recording information about the power of attorney if the notary does not know the information when the certificate is completed.[3] A notary's failure to adhere to this requirement does not invalidate the instrument, nor is it a permissible ground for a register to refuse to record a real estate instrument.[4]

The notary's certificate must be written on the document or permanently attached to it. Removable labels or stickers are unacceptable. When motor vehicle title documents are acknowledged, the acknowledgment must be on the document itself.

Some notaries add nonstatutory language to their certificates, such as "let the instrument with this certificate be registered" or a similar expression. This phrase is not required and has no legal significance.

Although substantial rather than exact compliance with most of the statutory forms is sufficient for legal validity, it is usually best to follow the wording provided. What may seem an inconsequential variation to the notary can actually be a problematic omission or alteration invalidating the certificate. Some alterations are appropriate, however, such as modifying references to male gender to reflect a female subject.

4.1.1 Acknowledgments

A certificate for an acknowledgment need not be in any precise language. It will be sufficient as long as it includes the following:[5]

- The state and county in which the acknowledgment occurred
- The name of the principal who appeared in person before the notary
- A statement that the principal appearing in person before the notary acknowledged that he or she signed the record
- The date of the acknowledgment

1. N.C. GEN. STAT. § 47-37.1 (hereinafter G.S.).
2. G.S. 10B-20(o).
3. G.S. 10B-20(o)(1).
4. G.S. 10B-20(o)(2), (3).
5. G.S. 10B-40(b).

- The notary's signature
- The notary's official seal
- The notary's commission expiration date

4.1.2 Verifications or Proofs

A certificate for a verification or proof need not be in any precise language. It will be sufficient as long as it includes the following:[6]

- The state and county in which the verification or proof occurred
- The name of the subscribing witness who appeared in person before the notary
- The name of the principal whose signature is to be verified or proven
- A statement that the subscribing witness certified to the notary under oath or by affirmation that the subscribing witness is not a party to or a beneficiary of the transaction, signed the record as a subscribing witness, and witnessed either the principal sign the record or acknowledge the principal's signature on the already-signed record
- The date of the verification or proof
- The notary's signature
- The notary's official seal
- The notary's commission expiration date

4.1.3 Oaths or Affirmations

A certificate for an oath or affirmation need not be in any precise language. It will be sufficient as long as it includes the following:[7]

- The name of the principal who appeared in person before the notary and gave the oath or affirmation unless the name is otherwise clear from the record
- A statement that the principal who appeared in person before the notary signed the record in question and certified to the notary under oath or by affirmation as to the truth of the matters stated in the record
- The date of the oath or affirmation
- The notary's signature
- The notary's official seal
- The notary's commission expiration date

Note that unlike a certificate for an attestation or a verification or proof, a certificate for an oath or affirmation is not required to contain the state and county in which the notarial act occurred.

4.2 Basic Forms: Notary Act

The North Carolina Notary Act provides basic forms of certificates for acknowledgments, verifications or proofs, and oaths or affirmations, which are set forth below. The Notary Act provides that these forms are sufficient to satisfy the requirements for the notarial acts

---

6. G.S. 10B-40(c).
7. G.S. 10B-40(d).

they certify. The statutes contain numerous other forms of certificates for par
ment types. Notaries may find that those who prepare documents may pref
certificates to address particular formalities associated with the subject ma
these specialized certificates are also set forth below. In any event, it is no
responsibility to give advice about which certificate is most appropriate for a specific purpose; rather, the notary is to ensure that the certificate he or she completes contains the
minimum elements required by law for a particular notarial act.

4.2.1 Basic Acknowledgment Certificate

The North Carolina Notary Act provides a form of notarial certificate for an acknowledgment. If the certificate is substantially in the statutory form, its completion signifies that
the notary has ensured compliance with the following requirements, even if these requirements are not explicitly set out in the certificate:

- The principal acknowledged his or her signature.
- The principal appeared in person before the notary and presented a record.
- The principal signed the record in the notary's presence or indicated to the
  notary that the signature on the record is the principal's.
- The notary has either personal knowledge of the principal's identity or satisfactory evidence of the principal's identity as required by law (see section
  3.2.2 above).[8]

The following is the Notary Act form of notarial certificate for the acknowledgment of
one or more principals acting in their own right or in a representative or fiduciary capacity. When an instrument is executed by two or more persons and their acknowledgments
are taken at different times, a separate certificate will be necessary for each. A certificate
is sufficient if it complies substantially with this form or with another form allowed by
law.[9]

---

county in which acknowledgment taken County, North Carolina

     I certify that the following person(s) personally appeared before me this day, each
acknowledging to me that he or she signed the foregoing document: *name(s) of
principals*.

Date: *date of acknowledgment*

(Official Seal)   *official signature of notary*
                                        notary's printed or typed name, Notary Public
                                        My commission expires: *date commission expires*

---

8. G.S. 10B-3(1); G.S. 10B-40(a1)(1).
9. G.S. 10B-41(a).

4.2.1.1 Example: Individual in Own Behalf

The following is an example of the Notary Act acknowledgment certificate for one individual signing for him- or herself:

On March 15, 2006, Mary Jones appeared before John Allen Smith, an Orange County notary, to execute a deed. Smith's commission expires April 15, 2008. The acknowledgment was taken in Wake County.

Wake County, North Carolina   *Mary Jones*

I certify that the following person(s) personally appeared before me this day, each acknowledging to me that he or she signed the foregoing document: Mary Jones.

Date: March 15, 2006   *John Allen Smith*

                            John Allen Smith, Notary Public
                            My commission expires: April 15, 2008

[NOTARY PUBLIC seal: John Allen Smith, Orange County, NC]

4.2.1.2 Example: Two or More Individuals for Themselves

The following is an example of the Notary Act acknowledgment certificate when two or more individuals sign for themselves:

On March 15, 2006, Mary Jones and Robert Morris appeared before John Allen Smith, an Orange County notary, to execute a deed. Smith's commission expires April 15, 2008. The acknowledgment was taken in Wake County.

                                    Mary Jones
Wake County, North Carolina   *Robert Morris*

I certify that the following person(s) personally appeared before me this day, each acknowledging to me that he or she signed the foregoing document: Mary Jones and Robert Morris.

Date: March 15, 2006   *John Allen Smith*

                            John Allen Smith, Notary Public
                            My commission expires: April 15, 2008

[NOTARY PUBLIC seal: John Allen Smith, Orange County, NC]

4.2.1.3 Example: Representative or Fiduciary Capacity

An individual who signs in a representative or fiduciary capacity is deemed by law to have the capacity indicated.[10] A notary is not required to verify this authority.[11] A notary may, but is not required to, indicate in the certificate a statement that the individual signed as a representative or fiduciary (for example, "as President"), or that the individual had due authority to sign (for example, "as President of Acme Corporation, duly authorized"), or the notary may include a simple reference to the individual's capacity (for example, "as President of Acme Corporation").[12] When an instrument signed in a representative capacity is to be recorded with the register of deeds, the certificate may state that the individual was acting in a representative capacity or was duly authorized to do so, and the certificate may identify the represented person or entity.[13] There is no requirement, however, to include this information in the certificate in all cases.[14]

The following is an example of the Notary Act acknowledgment certificate for an individual signing in a representative or fiduciary capacity, such as when the principal is an officer of a corporation or limited liability company:

> On March 15, 2006, Mary Jones appeared before John Allen Smith, an Orange County notary, to execute a deed. She signed as president of Acme Corporation. Smith's commission expires April 15, 2008. The acknowledgment was taken in Wake County.

ACME CORPORATION

Mary Jones

President

Wake County, North Carolina

I certify that the following person(s) personally appeared before me this day, each acknowledging to me that he or she signed the foregoing document: Mary Jones, as President of Acme Corporation.

Date: March 15, 2006

John Allen Smith

John Allen Smith, Notary Public
My commission expires: April 15, 2008

[Notary Seal: John Allen Smith — NOTARY PUBLIC — Orange County, NC]

Other common forms of representative or fiduciary capacity include other officers on behalf of a corporation, a general partner on behalf of a partnership or limited partnership, a manager on behalf of a limited liability company, and a trustee on behalf of a

---

10. G.S. 10B-40(h).
11. G.S. 10B-40(h).
12. G.S. 10B-40(h).
13. G.S. 47-37.1(b).
14. G.S. 47-37.1(b).

trust or an association. Execution by an ecclesiastical officer, such as a minister or bishop, designated by a religious group to administer its affairs, is acknowledged or proved in the same manner, with the capacity indicated. Chapter 5, "Common Notarial Settings," discusses other frequently encountered types of organizations.

An individual who uses an assumed or "doing business as" ("d/b/a") name is not signing in a representative capacity, but he or she may indicate the assumed name as well as the proper name. In that case, the certificate could indicate both the real name and the assumed name, as in the following example:

> I certify that the following person(s) personally appeared before me this day, each acknowledging to me that he or she voluntarily signed the foregoing document for the purpose stated therein: *Mary Jones, d/b/a Mary Jones Records.*

4.2.2 Basic Verification or Proof Certificate

The North Carolina Notary Act provides a form of notarial certificate for a verification or proof. If the certificate is substantially in the statutory form, its completion signifies that the notary ensured compliance with the following requirements, even if these requirements are not explicitly set out in the certificate:

- The individual appeared in person before the notary.
- The individual certified to the notary under oath or by affirmation that he or she is not a party to or a beneficiary of the transaction.
- The individual gave an oath or affirmation to one of the following:
  1. The individual is a subscribing witness who personally observed a principal sign the record;
  2. The individual is a subscribing witness to whom a principal acknowledged having signed the record; or
  3. The individual recognizes a signature by a principal or subscribing witness to be genuine.
- The notary has either personal knowledge of the subscribing witness's identity or satisfactory evidence of the subscribing witness's identity as required by law (see section 3.2.2 above).[15]

The following is the Notary Act form of notarial certificate for a verification or proof of the signature of a principal by a subscribing witness. A certificate is sufficient if it complies substantially with this form or with another form allowed by law.[16]

---

15. G.S. 10B-3(28); G.S. 10B-40(a1)(4).
16. G.S. 10B-42(a).

---

county in which verification or proof taken County, North Carolina

    I certify that *name of subscribing witness* personally appeared before me this day and certified to me under oath or by affirmation that he or she is not a grantee or beneficiary of the transaction, signed the foregoing document as a subscribing witness, and either (i) witnessed *name of principal* sign the foregoing document or (ii) witnessed *name of principal* acknowledge his or her signature on the already-signed document.

Date: *date of verification or proof*

(Official Seal)   *official signature of notary*
                                      notary's printed or typed name, Notary Public
                                    My commission expires: *date commission expires*

The following is an example of the Notary Act certificate for a verification or proof:

On March 15, 2006, Robert Samuel Washington appeared before John Allen Smith, an Orange County notary, to certify that he witnessed Mary Jones sign a document. Washington gave an oath that he is not a grantee or beneficiary of the transaction. Smith's commission expires April 15, 2008. The proof occurred in Wake County.

Witness to signature of Mary Jones: *Mary Jones*
                                            Robert Samuel Washington

Wake County, North Carolina

    I certify that Robert Samuel Washington personally appeared before me this day and certified to me under oath or by affirmation that he or she is not a grantee or beneficiary of the transaction, signed the foregoing document as a subscribing witness, and either (i) witnessed Mary Jones sign the foregoing document or (ii) witnessed Mary Jones acknowledge his or her signature on the already-signed document.

Date: March 15, 2006   *John Allen Smith*
                                      John Allen Smith, Notary Public
                                      My commission expires: April 15, 2008

(Notary seal: John Allen Smith / NOTARY PUBLIC / Orange County, NC)

The following is the Notary Act form of notarial certificate for a verification or proof by a nonsubscribing witness. In this situation someone gives an oath or affirmation about recognizing a signature by a principal or subscribing witness, but the person giving the oath or affirmation does not sign the document. A certificate is sufficient if it complies substantially with this form or with another form allowed by law.[17]

---

county in which verification or proof taken County, North Carolina

I certify *name of nonsubscribing witness* personally appeared before me this day and certified to me under oath or by affirmation that he or she is not a grantee or beneficiary of the transaction, that *name of nonsubscribing witness* recognizes the signature of *name of the principal or the subscribing witness* and that the signature is genuine.

Date: *date of verification or proof*

(Official Seal)   *official signature of notary*
                                                   notary's printed or typed name, Notary Public
                                                   My commission expires: *date commission expires*

The following is an example of the Notary Act certificate for a verification or proof of a signature by a nonsubscribing witness:

> On March 15, 2006, Robert Samuel Washington appeared before John Allen Smith, an Orange County notary, to testify that he recognizes the signature of Mary Jones to be genuine. Washington gave an oath that he is not a grantee or beneficiary of the transaction. Smith's commission expires April 15, 2008. The proof occurred in Wake County.

Wake County, North Carolina

I certify Robert Samuel Washington personally appeared before me this day and certified to me under oath or by affirmation that he or she is not a grantee or beneficiary of the transaction, that Robert Samuel Washington recognizes the signature of Mary Jones and that the signature is genuine.

Date: March 15, 2006

John Allen Smith, Notary Public
My commission expires: April 15, 2008

---

17. G.S. 10B-42.1.

4.2.3 Basic Oath or Affirmation Certificate

The North Carolina Notary Act provides a form of notarial certificate for an oath or affirmation. The form also is sufficient for a jurat. If the certificate is substantially in the statutory form, its completion signifies that the notary ensured compliance with the following requirements, even if these requirements are not explicitly set out in the certificate:

- The principal appeared in person before the notary.
- The principal made a vow of truthfulness on penalty of perjury by oath or affirmation.
- The notary has either personal knowledge of the principal's identity or satisfactory evidence of the principal's identity as required by law (see section 3.2.2 above).[18]

The Notary Act provides two forms of certificate for an oath or affirmation. A certificate is sufficient if it complies substantially with either form or with another form allowed by law.[19] The first form is as follows:

---

county in which oath or affirmation given County, North Carolina

Signed and sworn to before me this day by *name of principal*.

Date: *date of oath or affirmation*

(Official Seal)   *official signature of notary*
                                            notary's printed or typed name, Notary Public
                                            My commission expires: *date commission expires*

The second of the two forms is as follows:

---

county in which oath or affirmation given County, North Carolina

Sworn to and subscribed before me this day by *name of principal*.

Date: *date of oath or affirmation*

(Official Seal)   *official signature of notary*
                                            notary's printed or typed name, Notary Public
                                            My commission expires: *date commission expires*

The words "affirmed" or "sworn to or affirmed" should be substituted for the words "sworn to" if an affirmation is given rather than an oath.[20] The principal's name need not be recited in the certificate text if it appears near the certificate and is clear from the record.[21]

---

18. G.S. 10B-3(2), (14); G.S. 10B-40(a1)(2), (3).
19. G.S. 10B-43(a).
20. G.S. 10B-43(d)(2).
21. G.S. 10B-43(d)(1).

The following is an example of the Notary Act certificate for an oath or affirmation:

On March 15, 2006, Mary Jones swore to the contents of an affidavit before John Allen Smith, an Orange County notary. Smith's commission expires April 15, 2008. The oath was given in Wake County.

Mary Jones

Wake County, North Carolina

Signed and sworn to before me this day by Mary Jones.

Date: March 15, 2006

John Allen Smith

John Allen Smith, Notary Public
My commission expires: April 15, 2008

[Notary seal: John Allen Smith / NOTARY PUBLIC / Orange County, NC]

4.3 Alternative Statutory Forms of Certificates for Real Estate Instruments

The statutes governing the registration of real estate instruments, G.S. Chapter 47, provide a number of certificate forms. These forms may be used as alternatives to the Notary Act forms described above.

4.3.1 Acknowledgment

The statutes governing real estate instruments provide the following alternative certificate form appropriate for an instrument acknowledged by one or more individuals acting in an individual, representative, or fiduciary capacity.[22]

---

22. G.S. 47-38.

North Carolina, _county in which acknowledgment taken_ County

    I, _notary's printed or typed name_, a Notary Public for _county of notary's commission_ County, North Carolina, do hereby certify that _name of person whose acknowledgment is taken_ personally appeared before me this day and acknowledged the due execution of the foregoing instrument.

Witness my hand and official seal this the _day of acknowledgment_ day of _month of acknowledgment_, _year of acknowledgment_.

(Official Seal)

                                     official signature of notary

                                     My commission expires: _date commission expires_

This form can be used by representatives or fiduciaries in their many capacities, such as individuals acting for an unincorporated association, managers or members acting for a limited liability company, the trustee of a trust, or a guardian for a minor.

    The following is an example of the alternative real estate instrument acknowledgment for one individual signing for him- or herself:

> On March 15, 2006, Mary Jones appeared before John Allen Smith, an Orange County notary, to execute a deed. Smith's commission expires April 15, 2008. The acknowledgment was taken in Wake County.

Mary Jones

North Carolina, Wake County

    I, John Allen Smith, a Notary Public for Orange County, North Carolina, do hereby certify that Mary Jones personally appeared before me this day and acknowledged the due execution of the foregoing instrument.

Witness my hand and official seal this the 15th day of March, 2006.

John Allen Smith

My commission expires: April 15, 2008

(Seal: John Allen Smith — NOTARY PUBLIC — Orange County, NC)

4.3.2 Acknowledgment by Two or More Persons

The statutes provide the following alternative form for an acknowledgment of a real estate instrument by a husband and wife or by two or more other grantors.[23] When an instrument is executed by two or more persons and their acknowledgments are taken at different times, separate certificates for each acknowledgment, as shown in the previous example, will be necessary instead.

North Carolina, *county in which acknowledgment taken* County

    I, *notary's printed or typed name*, a Notary Public for *county of notary's commission* County, North Carolina, do hereby certify that *name of persons whose acknowledgments are taken* personally appeared before me this day and acknowledged the due execution of the foregoing (or annexed) instrument.

Witness my hand and official seal this the *day of acknowledgment* day of *month of acknowledgment*, *year of acknowledgment*.

(Official Seal)   *official signature of notary*

                                My commission expires: *date commission expires*

    The following is an example of the alternative real estate instrument acknowledgment for two or more individuals signing for themselves:

> On March 15, 2006, Mary Jones and Robert Morris appeared before John Allen Smith, an Orange County notary, to execute a deed. Smith's commission expires April 15, 2008. The acknowledgment was taken in Wake County.

Mary Jones
Robert Morris

North Carolina, Wake County

    I, John Allen Smith, a Notary Public for Orange County, North Carolina, do hereby certify that Mary Jones and Robert Morris personally appeared before me this day and acknowledged the due execution of the foregoing (or annexed) instrument.

Witness my hand and official seal this the 15th day of March, 2006.

                         John Allen Smith

John Allen Smith
NOTARY PUBLIC
Orange County, NC

                         My commission expires: April 15, 2008

---

23. G.S. 47-40.

4.3.3 Proof by Subscribing Witness

The statutes provide the following alternative form for an instrument proved by a subscribing witness:[24]

STATE OF NORTH CAROLINA
county in which proof occurs COUNTY

    I, *notary's printed or typed name*, a Notary Public of *county of notary's commission* County, North Carolina, certify that *name of subscribing witness* personally appeared before me this day, and being duly sworn, stated in his presence *name of principal* (signed the foregoing instrument) (acknowledged the execution of the foregoing instrument). (Strike out the words not applicable.)

    WITNESS my hand and official seal this the *day of proof* day of *month of proof, year of proof.*

(Official Seal)   *official signature of notary*
                                   Notary Public
                                   My commission expires: *date commission expires*

    The following is an example of a certificate made upon proof of an instrument by a subscribing witness:

    On March 15, 2006, Robert Samuel Washington appeared before John Allen Smith, an Orange County notary, to testify that he witnessed Mary Jones sign a document. Washington gave an oath that he is not named in the document and has no interest in the transaction. Smith's commission expires April 15, 2008. The proof occurred in Wake County.

Witness to signature of Mary Jones: *Robert Samuel Washington*

STATE OF NORTH CAROLINA
WAKE COUNTY

    I, John Allen Smith, a Notary Public of Orange County, North Carolina, certify that Robert Samuel Washington personally appeared before me this day, and being duly sworn, stated in his presence Mary Jones (signed the foregoing instrument) ~~(acknowledged the execution of the foregoing instrument). (Strike out the words not applicable.)~~

WITNESS my hand and official seal this the 15th day of March, 2006.

(Official Seal)   *John Allen Smith*
               Notary Public
               My commission expires: April 15, 2008

---

24. G.S. 47-43.2.

4.4 Alternative Statutory Forms for Entity Conveyances of Real Estate

The Notary Act forms depicted in section 4.2.1.3 for acknowledgment of a signature in a representative capacity are sufficient for real estate conveyances made by corporations. North Carolina statutes governing real estate registration provide alternative forms of corporate acknowledgments for signatures on deeds and other conveyances. These alternative forms are described below. Some forms include a reference to a corporate seal. These seals are no longer required for real estate conveyances,[25] and the phrase "sealed with its corporate seal" should be omitted from a certificate if the seal of the corporation has not been affixed to the instrument being acknowledged.[26]

These forms may be modified and adapted for use for certificates for other entities, such as for general and limited partnerships, limited liability companies, trusts, and unincorporated associations.[27] In such circumstances the appropriate substitutions would be made to references in the certificate to the nature of the entity and the individual's capacity.

4.4.1 Acknowledgment by Corporate Officer Designated by Statute or Corporate Resolution

The following form may be used when a corporate officer executes the instrument without a corporate seal or attestation by another corporate officer.[28] The signing official must be the corporation's chairman, president, chief executive officer, vice president or assistant vice president, treasurer, chief financial officer, or any other agent authorized by a signed and attested resolution of the corporation's board of directors.[29]

North Carolina
county in which acknowledgment taken County

    I, _notary's printed or typed name_, Notary Public for _county of notary's commission_ County, North Carolina, certify that _name of corporate officer_ personally came before me this day and acknowledged that he (or she) is _title of corporate officer_ of _name of corporation_, a corporation, and that he/she, as _title of corporate officer_, being authorized to do so, executed the foregoing on behalf of the corporation.

    Witness my hand and official seal, this the _day of acknowledgment_ day of _month of acknowledgment_, _year of acknowledgment_.

official signature of notary
My commission expires: _date commission expires_

(Official Seal)

The following is an example of the alternative statutory form of corporate acknowledgment of a signature by an authorized officer:

---

25. G.S. 39-6.5.
26. G.S. 47-41.01(d)(6).
27. G.S. 47-41.01(e); G.S. 47-41.02(h).
28. G.S. 47-41.01(c).
29. G.S. 47-18.3(e); G.S. 47-41.01(d)(4).

On March 15, 2006, Mary Jones appeared before John Allen Smith, an Orange County notary, to execute a deed. She signed as president of Acme Corporation. Smith's commission expires April 15, 2008. The acknowledgment was taken in Wake County.

ACME CORPORATION

Mary Jones

President

Wake County, North Carolina

I, John Allen Smith, a Notary Public for Orange County, North Carolina, certify that Mary Jones personally came before me this day and acknowledged that he (or she) is president of Acme Corporation, a corporation, and that he/she, as president, being authorized to do so, executed the foregoing on behalf of the corporation.

Witness my hand and official seal, this the 15th day of March, 2006.

John Allen Smith

My commission expires: April 15, 2008

[SEAL: John Allen Smith / NOTARY PUBLIC / Orange County, NC]

4.4.2 Acknowledgment by Attesting Corporate Officer, with Corporate Seal and Other Executive Officer Signature

The following form may be used when an instrument has been executed by a corporate official, a corporate seal is affixed, and a second corporate official attests to the execution of the instrument.[30] Only the attesting officer need appear before the notary.

The attesting officer whose signature is acknowledged must be the corporation's secretary or assistant secretary, trust officer, assistant trust officer, associate trust officer, or in the case of a bank, its secretary, assistant secretary, cashier, or assistant cashier.[31] The other officer whose signature appears must be the corporation's chairman, president, chief executive officer, vice president or assistant vice president, treasurer, chief financial officer, or any other agent authorized by a signed and attested resolution of the corporation's board of directors.[32]

---

30. G.S. 47-41.01(b).
31. G.S. 47-41.01(d)(5).
32. G.S. 47-18.3(e); G.S. 47-41.01(d)(4).

North Carolina
county in which acknowledgment taken County

    I, *notary's printed or typed name*, a Notary Public for *county of notary's commission* County, North Carolina, certify that *name of attesting corporate official* personally came before me this day and acknowledged that he (or she) is *title of attesting corporate official* of *name of corporation*, a corporation, and that by authority duly given and as the act of the corporation, the foregoing instrument was signed in its name by *title of officer whose signature is being attested*, sealed with its corporate seal, and attested by himself (or herself) as its *title of attesting corporate official*.

Witness my hand and official seal, this the *day of acknowledgment* day of *month of acknowledgment*, *year of acknowledgment*.

        official signature of notary

(Official Seal)   My commission expires: *date commission expires*

    The following is an example of the alternative statutory form for a corporate verification by an authorized attesting corporate official of an authorized officer's signature, with the corporate seal:

    On March 15, 2006, Robert Samuel Washington appeared before John Allen Smith, an Orange County notary. Washington is the secretary of Acme Corporation. He attested to the signature of Mary Jones, who is the president of Acme Corporation. Smith's commission expires April 15, 2008. The acknowledgment was taken in Wake County.

ACME CORPORATION

President

Attested: Secretary

North Carolina
Wake County

    I, John Allen Smith, a Notary Public for Orange County, North Carolina, certify that Robert Samuel Washington personally came before me this day and acknowledged that he (or she) is secretary of Acme Corporation, a corporation, and that by authority duly given and as the act of the corporation, the foregoing instrument was signed in its name by its president, sealed with its corporate seal, and attested by himself (or herself) as its secretary.

Witness my hand and official seal, this the 15th day of March, 2006.

My commission expires: April 15, 2008

4.4.3 Proof by Secretary or Assistant Secretary of Execution by President, Presiding Member, or Trustee, with Corporate Seal

The following form may be used when an instrument has been executed by the president, presiding member, or trustee of the corporation and a corporate seal affixed. The corporate secretary or assistant secretary attests under oath to the execution of the instrument:[33]

North Carolina
county in which proof occurs County

    This _day of proof_ day of _month of proof_, A.D. _year of proof_, personally came before me _notary's printed or typed name_, a Notary Public for _county of notary's commission_ County, North Carolina, _name of attesting corporate secretary or assistant secretary_, who, being by me duly sworn, says that he knows the common seal of _name of corporation_, and is acquainted with _name of president, presiding member, or trustee whose signature is being attested_, who is the president of said corporation, and that he, the said _name of attesting corporate secretary or assistant secretary_, is the secretary (or assistant secretary) of the said corporation, and saw the said president sign the foregoing (or annexed) instrument, and saw the said common seal of said corporation affixed to said instrument by said president (or that he, the said _name of attesting corporate secretary or assistant secretary_, secretary or assistant secretary as aforesaid, affixed said seal to said instrument), and that he, the said _name of attesting corporate secretary or assistant secretary_, signed his name in attestation of the execution of said instrument in the presence of said president of said corporation. Witness my hand and official seal, this _day of proof_ day of _month of proof_, _year of proof_.

(Official Seal)   _official signature of notary_
                                 My commission expires: _date commission expires_

The following is an example of the alternative statutory form of a corporate certificate of an attesting secretary or assistant secretary of the execution of an instrument by the president, presiding member, or trustee of the corporation, with the corporate seal:

> On March 15, 2006, Robert Samuel Washington appeared before John Allen Smith, an Orange County notary. Washington is the secretary of Acme Corporation. He is attesting to the signature of Mary Jones, the president of Acme Corporation, and gives an oath that he witnessed the signature and the affixing of the corporate seal. Smith's commission expires April 15, 2008. The proof occurred in Wake County.

---

33. G.S. 47-41.02(c).

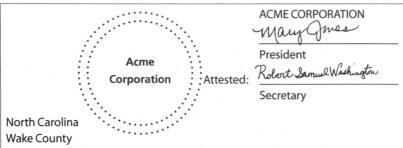

ACME CORPORATION

Mary Jones

President

Attested: *Robert Samuel Washington*

Secretary

North Carolina
Wake County

    This 15th day of March, A.D. 2006, personally came before me John Allen Smith, a Notary Public for Orange County, North Carolina, Robert Samuel Washington, who, being by me duly sworn, says that he knows the common seal of Acme Corporation, and is acquainted with Mary Jones who is the president of said corporation, and that he, the said Robert Samuel Washington, is the secretary (or assistant secretary) of the said corporation, and saw the said president sign the foregoing (or annexed) instrument, and saw the said common seal of said corporation affixed to said instrument by said president (or that he, the said Robert Samuel Washington, secretary or assistant secretary as aforesaid, affixed said seal to said instrument), and that he, the said Robert Samuel Washington, signed his name in attestation of the execution of said instrument in the presence of said president of said corporation. Witness my hand and official seal, this 15th day of March, 2006.

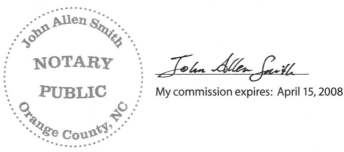

John Allen Smith

My commission expires: April 15, 2008

4.4.4 Proof by President, Vice President, Presiding Member, or Trustee with Attestation by Secretary or Assistant Secretary, with Corporate Seal

The following form may be used when an instrument has been executed by the president, vice president, presiding member, or trustee of a corporation and attested to by the secretary or assistant secretary. The person who executed the instrument must give an oath before the notary, and the corporate seal must be affixed to the document:[34]

---

34. G.S. 47-41.02(d).

North Carolina
county in which proof occurs County

    This _day of proof_ day of _month of proof_, _year of proof_, personally came before me _notary's printed or typed name_, Notary Public for _county of notary's commission_ County, North Carolina, _name of corporate president, vice president, presiding member, or trustee who signed_, who, being by me duly sworn, says that he is _signer's title—president, vice president, presiding member, or trustee_ of _name of corporation_, and that the seal affixed to the foregoing (or annexed) instrument in writing is the corporate seal of said company, and that said writing was signed and sealed by him in behalf of said corporation by its authority duly given. And the said _name of corporate president, vice president, presiding member, or trustee who signed_ acknowledged the said writing to be the act and deed of said corporation.

(Official Seal)

                                          official signature of notary
                                        My commission expires: _date commission expires_

    The following is an example of the alternative statutory form for a corporate proof by the president, vice president, presiding member, or trustee of the corporation, with the secretary or assistant secretary's attestation and a corporate seal affixed:

    On March 15, 2006, Mary Jones appeared before John Allen Smith, an Orange County notary, to acknowledge having signed a deed. She is president of Acme Corporation. She gave an oath about the truth of the matters stated in the certificate. The corporate seal is on the document as is the signature of Robert Samuel Washington, the secretary of the corporation. Smith's commission expires April 15, 2008. The proof occurred in Wake County.

ACME CORPORATION

Mary Jones
President

Attested: _Robert Samuel Washington_
Secretary

(Acme Corporation seal)

North Carolina
Wake County

    This 15th day of March, 2006, personally came before me John Allen Smith, Notary Public for Orange County, North Carolina, Mary Jones who, being by me duly sworn, says that she is president of Acme Corporation, and that the seal affixed to the foregoing (or annexed) instrument in writing is the corporate seal of said company, and that said writing was signed and sealed by her in behalf of said corporation by its authority duly given. And the said Mary Jones acknowledged the said writing to be the act and deed of said corporation.

John Allen Smith
My commission expires: April 15, 2008

(Notary seal: John Allen Smith, NOTARY PUBLIC, Orange County, NC)

4.4.5 Proof by Subscribing Witness under Oath of Execution by President, Presiding Member, or Trustee and Signatures of Two Other Members of Corporation, with Corporate Seal

The following form may be used when an instrument has been executed by the president, presiding member, or trustee of a corporation before a subscribing witness and two other members of the corporation. The subscribing witness gives an oath before the notary that the subscribing witness observed the signing of the document and the affixing of the corporate seal and that the subscribing witness knows the individuals who signed the instrument and is familiar with the seal.[35]

North Carolina, *county in which proof occurs* County

    This *day of proof* day of *month of proof*, A.D. *year of proof*, personally came before me *notary's printed or typed name*, Notary Public for *county of notary's commission* County, North Carolina, *name of subscribing witness*, who, being by me duly sworn, says that he knows the common seal of the *name of corporation*, and is also acquainted with *name of corporate president, presiding member, or trustee who signed*, who is the president (or presiding member or trustee), and also with *name of first corporate member who is a witness* and *name of second corporate member who is a witness*, two other members of said corporation; and that he, the said *name of subscribing witness*, saw the said president (or presiding member or trustee) and the two said other members sign the said instrument, and saw the said president (or presiding member or trustee) affix the said common seal of said corporation thereto, and that he, the said subscribing witness, signed his name as such subscribing witness thereto in their presence. Witness my hand and official seal, this the *day of proof* day of *month of proof, year of proof*.

(Official Seal)

                                    official signature of notary
                                    My commission expires: *date commission expires*

    The following is an example of the alternative statutory form for a corporate proof by a subscribing witness under oath of a signature by the president, presiding member, or trustee of a corporation before two other corporate members, with all witnesses signing and the corporate seal affixed:

> On March 15, 2006, Robert Samuel Washington appeared before John Allen Smith, an Orange County notary, to attest to the signature of Mary Jones, president of Acme Corporation, before Cindy Harris and Joseph Carter, members of Acme Corporation. The corporate seal is affixed. Washington gave an oath before the notary that he saw the signatures made and knows the president and the other two witnesses and is familiar with the seal. Smith's commission expires April 15, 2008. The proof occurred in Wake County.

---

35. G.S. 47-41.02(b).

ACME CORPORATION

Mary Jones
President

Witness: *Cindy Harris*

Witness: *Joseph Carter*

Attested: *Robert Samuel Washington*

North Carolina, Wake County

This 15th day of March, A.D. 2006, personally came before me John Allen Smith, Notary Public for Orange County, North Carolina, Robert Samuel Washington, who, being by me duly sworn, says that he knows the common seal of the Acme Corporation, and is also acquainted with Mary Jones, who is the president (or presiding member or trustee), and also with Cindy Harris and Joseph Carter, two other members of said corporation; and that he, the said Robert Samuel Washington, saw the said president (or presiding member or trustee) and the two said other members sign the said instrument, and saw the said president (or presiding member or trustee) affix the said common seal of said corporation thereto, and that he, the said subscribing witness, signed his name as such subscribing witness thereto in their presence. Witness my hand and official seal, this the 15th day of March, 2006.

John Allen Smith

My commission expires:
April 15, 2008

4.5 Alternative Statutory Forms for Entity Conveyances of Personal Property

The statutes provide alternative forms of acknowledgment and proof for entity contracts for the conveyance of personal property.[36]

4.5.1 Acknowledgment by President, Secretary, or Treasurer

The following form is for acknowledgment of a signature by a corporation's president, secretary, or treasurer for a conveyance of corporate personal property:

---

36. G.S. 47-41.02(f).

North Carolina
county in which acknowledgment taken County

    I, _notary's printed or typed name_, a Notary Public for _county of notary's commission_ County, North Carolina, do hereby certify that _name of corporate president, secretary, or treasurer_ personally came before me this day and acknowledged that he is _title of president, secretary, or treasurer who signed_ of _name of corporation_ and acknowledged, on behalf of _name of corporation_, the grantor, the due execution of the foregoing instrument.

    Witness my hand and official seal, this the _day of acknowledgment_ day of _month of acknowledgment_, _year of acknowledgment_.

(Official Seal)

                                          official signature of notary
                                          My commission expires: _date commission expires_

    The following is an example of the alternative statutory form for a corporate acknowledgment of a conveyance of personal property, with the signature of the corporation's president, secretary, or treasurer:

> On March 15, 2006, Mary Jones appeared before John Allen Smith, an Orange County notary, to execute a contract for conveyance of corporate personal property. Jones acknowledged that she is president of Acme Corporation and is signing in that capacity. Smith's commission expires April 15, 2008. The acknowledgment was taken in Wake County.

                                     ACME CORPORATION

                                     Mary Jones
                                     President

North Carolina
Wake County

    I, John Allen Smith, a Notary Public for Orange County, North Carolina, do hereby certify that Mary Jones personally came before me this day and acknowledged that she is president of Acme Corporation and acknowledged, on behalf of Acme Corporation, the grantor, the due execution of the foregoing instrument.

    Witness my hand and official seal, this the 15th day of March, 2006.

                                       John Allen Smith
                                       My commission expires: April 15, 2008

(Official Seal: John Allen Smith — NOTARY PUBLIC — Orange County, NC)

4.5.2 Proof by Corporate Officer of Execution by President, Secretary, or Treasurer

This form is for a subscribing witness's proof of a signature by the president, secretary, or treasurer for a conveyance of corporate personal property:

North Carolina
county in which proof occurs County

   I, _notary's printed or typed name_, a Notary Public for _county of notary's commission_ County,
North Carolina, certify that _name of subscribing witness_ personally appeared before me, and being
duly sworn, stated that in his presence _name of corporate president, secretary, or treasurer who signed_
(signed the foregoing instrument) (acknowledged the execution of the foregoing instrument).
(Strike out the words not applicable.)

   Witness my hand and official seal, this the _day of proof_ day of _month of proof, year of proof_.

(Official Seal)   _official signature of notary_
                                            Notary Public
                                            My commission expires: _date commission expires_

   The following is an example of a subscribing witness's proof of a signature in the corporate form by the president, treasurer, or secretary for a corporate conveyance of personal property:

   On March 15, 2006, Robert Samuel Washington appeared before John Allen Smith, an Orange County notary, to verify Mary Jones's execution of a contract for the conveyance of corporate personal property. Jones is president of Acme Corporation and signed in that capacity. Smith's commission expires April 15, 2008. The proof occurred in Wake County.

ACME CORPORATION

Mary Jones

President

Robert Samuel Washington

Witness to signature of Mary Jones:

North Carolina
Wake County

I, John Allen Smith, a Notary Public for Orange County, North Carolina, certify that Robert Samuel Washington personally appeared before me, and being duly sworn, stated that in his presence Mary Jones ~~(signed the foregoing instrument)~~ ~~(acknowledged the execution of the foregoing instrument).(Strike out the words not applicable.)~~

Witness my hand and official seal, this the 15th day of March, 2006.

John Allen Smith

Notary Public
My commission expires:
April 15, 2008

4.6 Short-Form Powers of Attorney

G.S. 32A-1 sets out a statutory form for a power of attorney called a "Short Form of General Power of Attorney." A power of attorney in this form will contain a notice in its heading that it is granting powers as defined in Chapter 32A. The statutory form includes a notarial certificate.[37] During the notarial act, the principal must be placed under oath. The statutory form does not mention the notary's printed or typed name, but it should be added beneath the notary's signature as indicated below.

STATE OF NORTH CAROLINA, COUNTY OF *county in which oath given*

On this *day of oath* day of *month of oath*, *year of oath*, personally appeared before me, the said named *name of person executing power of attorney exactly as the name appears on the signature line* to me known and known to me to be the person described in and who executed the foregoing instrument and he (or she) acknowledged that he (or she) executed the same and being duly sworn by me, made oath that the statements in the foregoing instrument are true.

My Commission Expires: *date commission expires*

(Official Seal)

official signature of notary
notary's printed or typed name
Notary Public

---

37. G.S. 32A-1.

The following is an example of a certificate for execution of a power of attorney by the principal:

Mary Jones gave Thomas Adams a power of attorney. She appeared before John Allen Smith, an Orange County notary, on March 15, 2006. Smith's commission expires April 15, 2008. The oath was given in Wake County.

Mary Jones

STATE OF NORTH CAROLINA, COUNTY OF WAKE

On this 15th day of March, 2006, personally appeared before me, the said named Mary Jones, to me known and known to me to be the person described in and who executed the foregoing instrument and he (or she) acknowledged that he (or she) executed the same and being duly sworn by me, made oath that the statements in the foregoing instrument are true.

My Commission Expires: April 15, 2008

John Allen Smith

John Allen Smith
Notary Public

(Seal: John Allen Smith / NOTARY PUBLIC / Orange County, NC)

4.7 Acknowledgment by Attorney-in-Fact

Someone signing an instrument for another person under a power of attorney should indicate that capacity near the signature. The attorney-in-fact may sign the instrument either in the principal's name by the named attorney-in-fact or in the attorney-in-fact's name for the named principal, as illustrated in section 3.2.3.[38] The statute provides the following sufficient form of certificate.[39] This form requires a recording reference to the power of attorney. If the reference information is not yet available because the power of attorney instrument will be recorded together with the instrument being executed by the attorney-in-fact, the statute allows the lines for this information to be left blank until the information is completed upon recordation.[40]

---

38. G.S. 47-43.1.
39. G.S. 47-43.
40. G.S. 10B-20(o)(1).

North Carolina, *county in which oath given* County

I, *notary's printed or typed name*, a Notary Public for *county of notary's commission* County, North Carolina, do hereby certify that *name of attorney-in-fact*, attorney-in-fact for *name of principal*, personally appeared before me this day, and being by me duly sworn, says that he executed the foregoing and annexed instrument for and in behalf of *name of principal*, and that his authority to execute and acknowledge said instrument is contained in an instrument duly executed, acknowledged, and recorded in the office of *office in which recorded, including county and state of recordation* on the *day, month, and year of recordation*, and that this instrument was executed under and by virtue of the authority given by said instrument granting him power of attorney; that the said *name of attorney-in-fact* acknowledged the due execution of the foregoing and annexed instrument for the purposes therein expressed for and in behalf of the said *name of principal*.

WITNESS my hand and official seal, this the *day of oath* day of *month of oath*, *year of oath*.

(Official Seal)   *official signature of notary*

My commission expires: *date commission expires*

The following is an example of a certificate for an attorney-in-fact signature in the statutory form:

> On March 15, 2006, Thomas Adams, who has power of attorney to sign for Mary Jones, appeared before John Allen Smith, an Orange County notary, to execute a deed. Smith's commission expires April 15, 2008. The oath was given in Wake County. The power of attorney was recorded on January 5, 2006, in the Orange County Register of Deeds at Book 555, Page 55.

North Carolina, Wake County

Thomas Adams, as attorney-in-fact for Mary Jones

I, John Allen Smith, a Notary Public for Orange County, North Carolina, do hereby certify that Thomas Adams, attorney-in-fact for Mary Jones, personally appeared before me this day, and being by me duly sworn, says that he executed the foregoing and annexed instrument for and in behalf of Mary Jones, and that his authority to execute and acknowledge said instrument is contained in an instrument duly executed, acknowledged, and recorded in the office of the Orange County, North Carolina, Register of Deeds at Book 555, Page 55, on the 5th day of January, 2006, and that this instrument was executed under and by virtue of the authority given by said instrument granting him power of attorney; that the said Thomas Adams acknowledged the due execution of the foregoing and annexed instrument for the purposes therein expressed for and in behalf of the said Mary Jones.

WITNESS my hand and official seal, this the 15th day of March, 2006.

(Official Seal: John Allen Smith, NOTARY PUBLIC, Orange County, NC)

John Allen Smith

My commission expires: April 15, 2008

4.8 Estate Planning Documents

Estate planning documents usually have special certificate forms providing information about formalities of execution that may affect the document's enforceability.

4.8.1 Wills

An ordinary "attested will" is signed by two witnesses, and its execution need not be acknowledged or proved before a notary.[41] Such a will is unusual today because its probate requires testimony or other proof.[42] The common form of will is "self-proved," eliminating the need for the witnesses to appear at probate unless the will is contested. The self-proved will must include an oath or affirmation by the testator and the two witnesses about a number of conditions as stated in the certificate. The notary may want to read from the certificate when taking the oaths or affirmations to ensure that all the required matters are covered. The special statutory form is as follows:[43]

I, *testator's name*, the testator, sign my name to this instrument this *day of oath* day of *month of oath*, *year of oath*, and being first duly sworn, do hereby declare to the undersigned authority that I sign and execute this instrument as my last will and that I sign it willingly (or willingly direct another to sign for me), that I execute it as my free and voluntary act for the purposes therein expressed, and that I am eighteen years of age or older, of sound mind, and under no constraint or undue influence.

testator's signature

Testator

We, *first witness's name*, *second witness's name*, the witnesses, sign our names to this instrument, being first duly sworn, and do hereby declare to the undersigned authority that the testator signs and executes this instrument as his last will and that he signs it willingly (or willingly directs another to sign for him), and that each of us, in the presence and hearing of the testator, hereby signs this will as witness to the testator's signing, and to the best of our knowledge the testator is eighteen years of age or older, of sound mind, and under no constraint or undue influence.

first witness's signature

Witness

second witness's signature

Witness

THE STATE OF NORTH CAROLINA

COUNTY OF *county in which oath given*

Subscribed, sworn to and acknowledged before me by *testator's name*, the testator, and subscribed and sworn to before me by *first witness's name* and *second witness's name*, witnesses, this *day of oath* day of *month of oath*, *year of oath*.

(Official Seal)

official signature of notary
notary's printed or typed name
Notary Public
My commission expires: *date commission expires*

---

41. G.S. 31-3.3.
42. G.S. 31-18.1.
43. G.S. 31-11.6(a).

The following is an example of a certificate for a self-proved will:

On March 15, 2006, Mary Jones executed her will before John Allen Smith, an Orange County notary. Cindy Harris and Joseph Carter are witnesses. Jones, Harris, and Carter all gave oaths concerning the matters stated in the certificate. Smith's commission expires April 15, 2008. The oaths were given in Wake County.

I, Mary Jones, the testator, sign my name to this instrument this 15th day of March, 2006, and being first duly sworn, do hereby declare to the undersigned authority that I sign and execute this instrument as my last will and that I sign it willingly (or willingly direct another to sign for me), that I execute it as my free and voluntary act for the purposes therein expressed, and that I am eighteen years of age or older, of sound mind, and under no constraint or undue influence.

Mary Jones
Mary Jones
Testator

We, Cindy Harris, Joseph Carter, the witnesses, sign our names to this instrument, being first duly sworn, and do hereby declare to the undersigned authority that the testator signs and executes this instrument as her last will and that she signs it willingly (or willingly directs another to sign for her), and that each of us, in the presence and hearing of the testator, hereby signs this will as witness to the testator's signing, and to the best of our knowledge the testator is eighteen years of age or older, of sound mind, and under no constraint or undue influence.

Cindy Harris
Witness

Joseph Carter
Witness

THE STATE OF NORTH CAROLINA
COUNTY OF WAKE

Subscribed, sworn to and acknowledged before me by Mary Jones, the testator, and subscribed and sworn to before me by Cindy Harris and Joseph Carter, witnesses, this 15th day of March, 2006.

John Allen Smith
John Allen Smith, Notary Public
My commission expires: April 15, 2008

[Notary seal: John Allen Smith, NOTARY PUBLIC, Orange County, NC]

An ordinary will can be made self-proving if the testator and witnesses of an already executed and attested will come before a notary or other officer authorized to administer oaths and make the required acknowledgments and verifications for self-proved wills, under oath or by affirmation. The following statutory form of certificate describes the nature of the representations being made:[44]

STATE OF NORTH CAROLINA
COUNTY OF _county in which oath given_

     Before me, the undersigned authority, on this day personally appeared _testator's name_, and _first witness's name_ and _second witness's name_, known to me to be the testator and the witnesses, respectively, whose names are signed to the attached or foregoing instrument and, all of these persons being by me first duly sworn. The testator, declared to me and to the witnesses in my presence: That said instrument is his last will, that he had willingly signed or directed another to sign the same for him, and executed it in the presence of said witnesses as his free and voluntary act for the purposes therein expressed; or, that the testator signified that the instrument was his instrument by acknowledging to them his signature previously affixed thereto.

     The said witnesses stated before me that the foregoing will was executed and acknowledged by the testator as his last will in the presence of said witnesses who, in his presence and at his request, subscribed their names thereto as attesting witnesses and that the testator, at the time of the execution of said will, was over the age of 18 years and of sound and disposing mind and memory.

testator's signature
Testator

first witness's signature
Witness

second witness's signature
Witness

     Subscribed, sworn and acknowledged before me by _testator's name_, the testator, subscribed and sworn to before me by _first witness's name_ and _second witness's name_, witnesses, this _day of oath_ day of _month of oath_, _year of oath_.

     (Official Seal)   _official signature of notary_
                                         notary's printed or typed name
                                       Notary Public
                                       My commission expires: _date commission expires_

---

44. G.S. 31-11.6(b).

The following is an example of a certificate to make an ordinary will self-proving:

On March 15, 2006, Mary Jones, Cindy Harris, and Joseph Carter appeared before John Allen Smith, an Orange County notary. Mary Jones has a will she has previously signed. She asked Cindy Harris and Joseph Carter to witness her acknowledgment of her signature. Jones, Harris, and Carter all gave oaths concerning the matters stated in the certificate. Smith's commission expires April 15, 2008. The oaths were given in Wake County.

STATE OF NORTH CAROLINA
COUNTY OF WAKE

Before me, the undersigned authority, on this day personally appeared Mary Jones, and Cindy Harris and Joseph Carter, known to me to be the testator and the witnesses, respectively, whose names are signed to the attached or foregoing instrument and, all of these persons being by me first duly sworn. The testator, declared to me and to the witnesses in my presence: That said instrument is her last will, that she had willingly signed or directed another to sign the same for her, and executed it in the presence of said witnesses as her free and voluntary act for the purposes therein expressed; or, that the testator signified that the instrument was her instrument by acknowledging to them her signature previously affixed thereto.

The said witnesses stated before me that the foregoing will was executed and acknowledged by the testator as her last will in the presence of said witnesses who, in her presence and at her request, subscribed their names thereto as attesting witnesses and that the testator, at the time of the execution of said will, was over the age of 18 years and of sound and disposing mind and memory.

Mary Jones
_____
Testator

Cindy Harris
_____
Witness

Joseph Carter
_____
Witness

Subscribed, sworn and acknowledged before me by Mary Jones, the testator, subscribed and sworn to before me by Cindy Harris and Joseph Carter, witnesses, this 15th day of March, 2006.

John Allen Smith

John Allen Smith
NOTARY
PUBLIC
Orange County, NC

John Allen Smith
_____
John Allen Smith, Notary Public
My commission expires: April 15, 2008

4.8.2 Living Wills

The legislature has provided a means by which a person may state in writing that in the event of a terminal or incurable illness extraordinary efforts not be used to prolong his or her life. The statute calls this a Declaration of a Desire for a Natural Death, more popularly known as a living will. The declaration must be certified, and a notary is one of the officers who may certify it. The declarant and the witnesses must give oaths or affirmations concerning the matters described in the certificate.[45] The notary may want to read from the certificate when taking the oaths or affirmations to ensure that all the required matters are covered.

The following is the statutory notary's certificate form for a declaration of a desire for a natural death:

North Carolina
County of _county in which oath given_

Certificate

I, _notary's printed or typed name_, a Notary Public for _county of notary's commission_, North Carolina, hereby certify that _declarant's name_, the declarant, appeared before me and swore to me and to the witnesses in my presence that this instrument is his Declaration Of A Desire For A Natural Death, and that he had willingly and voluntarily made and executed it as his free act and deed for the purposes expressed in it.

I further certify that _first witness's name_ and _second witness's name_, witnesses, appeared before me and swore that they witnessed _declarant's name_, declarant, sign the attached declaration, believing him to be of sound mind; and also swore that at the time they witnessed the declaration (i) they were not related within the third degree to the declarant or to the declarant's spouse, and (ii) they did not know or have a reasonable expectation that they would be entitled to any portion of the estate of the declarant upon the declarant's death under any will of the declarant or codicil thereto then existing or under the Intestate Succession Act as it provides at that time, and (III) they were not a physician attending the declarant or an employee of an attending physician or an employee of a health facility in which the declarant was a patient or an employee of a nursing home or any group-care home in which the declarant resided, and (iv) they did not have a claim against the declarant. I further certify that I am satisfied as to the genuineness and due execution of the declaration.

This the _day of oath_ day of _month of oath_, _year of oath_.

(Official Seal)

official signature of notary
Notary Public for the County of _county of notary's commission_
My commission expires: _date commission expires_

The following is an example of a certificate for a declaration of a desire for a natural death in the statutory form:

> On March 15, 2006, Mary Jones executed a living will in the statutory form before Cindy Harris and Joseph Carter, witnesses, and John Allen Smith, an Orange County notary. Smith's commission expires April 15, 2008. Jones, Harris, and Carter all gave oaths concerning the matters stated in the certificate. The oaths were given in Wake County.

---

45. G.S. 90-321.

Mary Jones

I hereby state that the declarant, Mary Jones, being of sound mind signed the above declaration in my presence and that I am not related to the declarant by blood or marriage and that I do not know or have a reasonable expectation that I would be entitled to any portion of the estate of the declarant under any existing will or codicil of the declarant or as an heir under the Intestate Succession Act if the declarant died on this date without a will. I also state that I am not the declarant's attending physician or an employee of the declarant's attending physician, or an employee of a health facility in which the declarant is a patient or an employee of a nursing home or any group-care home where the declarant resides. I further state that I do not now have any claim against the declarant.

Witness: *Cindy Harris*

Witness: *Joseph Carter*

North Carolina
County of Wake

Certificate

I, John Allen Smith, a Notary Public for Orange County, North Carolina, hereby certify that Mary Jones, the declarant, appeared before me and swore to me and to the witnesses in my presence that this instrument is her Declaration Of A Desire For A Natural Death, and that she had willingly and voluntarily made and executed it as her free act and deed for the purposes expressed in it.

I further certify that Cindy Harris and Joseph Carter, witnesses, appeared before me and swore that they witnessed Mary Jones, declarant, sign the attached declaration, believing her to be of sound mind; and also swore that at the time they witnessed the declaration (i) they were not related within the third degree to the declarant or to the declarant's spouse, and (ii) they did not know or have a reasonable expectation that they would be entitled to any portion of the estate of the declarant upon the declarant's death under any will of the declarant or codicil thereto then existing or under the Intestate Succession Act as it provides at that time, and (iii) they were not a physician attending the declarant or an employee of an attending physician or an employee of a health facility in which the declarant was a patient or an employee of a nursing home or any group-care home in which the declarant resided, and (iv) they did not have a claim against the declarant. I further certify that I am satisfied as to the genuineness and due execution of the declaration.

This the 15th day of March, 2006.

John Allen Smith

NOTARY PUBLIC
John Allen Smith
Orange County, NC

Notary Public for the County of Orange
My commission expires: April 15, 2008

4.8.3 Health Care Power of Attorney

There is a statutory form by which a person may designate an attorney-in-fact to deal with health care issues, such as the use of extraordinary measures in the event of a terminal illness, organ donations, or disposition of the body, on that person's behalf.[46] The form requires two witnesses. The declarant and the witnesses must give oaths or affirmations concerning the matters stated in the certificate. The notary may want to read from the certificate when taking the oaths or affirmations to ensure that all the required matters are covered.

STATE OF NORTH CAROLINA
COUNTY OF _county in which oath given_

CERTIFICATE

I, _notary's printed or typed name_, a Notary Public for _county of notary's commission_ North Carolina, hereby certify that _principal's name_ appeared before me and swore to me and to the witnesses in my presence that this instrument is a health care power of attorney, and that he/she willingly and voluntarily made and executed it as his/her free act and deed for the purposes expressed in it.

I further certify that _first witness's name_ and _second witness's name_, witnesses, appeared before me and swore that they witnessed _principal's name_ sign the attached health care power of attorney, believing him/her to be of sound mind; and also swore that at the time they witnessed the signing (i) they were not related within the third degree to him/her or his/her spouse, and (ii) they did not know nor have a reasonable expectation that they would be entitled to any portion of his/her estate upon his/her death under any will or codicil thereto then existing or under the Intestate Succession Act as it provided at that time, and (iii) they were not a physician attending him/her, nor an employee of an attending physician, nor an employee of a health facility in which he/she was a patient, nor an employee of a nursing home or any group-care home in which he/she resided, and (iv) they did not have a claim against him/her. I further certify that I am satisfied as to the genuineness and due execution of the instrument.

This the _day of oath_ day of _month of oath_, _year of oath_.

(Official Seal)   _official signature of notary_
                                            Notary Public
                                            My commission expires: _date commission expires_

The following is an example of the statutory form of certificate for a health care power of attorney executed before a notary by the declarant and two witnesses:

> On March 15, 2006, Mary Jones executed a health care power of attorney in the statutory form before Cindy Harris and Joseph Carter, witnesses, and John Allen Smith, an Orange County notary. Smith's commission expires April 15, 2008. Jones, Harris, and Carter all gave oaths concerning the matters stated in the certificate. The oaths were given in Wake County.

---

46. G.S. 32A-25.

Mary Jones

I hereby state that the Principal, Mary Jones, being of sound mind, signed the foregoing health care power of attorney in my presence, and that I am not related to the principal by blood or marriage, and I would not be entitled to any portion of the estate of the principal under any existing will or codicil of the principal or as an heir under the Intestate Succession Act, if the principal died on this date without a will. I also state that I am not the principal's attending physician, nor an employee of the principal's attending physician, nor an employee of the health facility in which the principal is a patient, nor an employee of a nursing home or any group-care home where the principal resides. I further state that I do not have any claim against the principal.

Witness: *Cindy Harris* _____ Date: March 15, 2006

Witness: *Joseph Carter* _____ Date: March 15, 2006

STATE OF NORTH CAROLINA
COUNTY OF WAKE

CERTIFICATE

I, John Allen Smith, a Notary Public for Orange County, North Carolina, hereby certify that Mary Jones appeared before me and swore to me and to the witnesses in my presence that this instrument is a health care power of attorney, and that he/she willingly and voluntarily made and executed it as his/her free act and deed for the purposes expressed in it.

I further certify that Cindy Harris and Joseph Carter, witnesses, appeared before me and swore that they witnessed Mary Jones sign the attached health care power of attorney, believing him/her to be of sound mind; and also swore that at the time they witnessed the signing (i) they were not related within the third degree to him/her or his/her spouse, and (ii) they did not know nor have a reasonable expectation that they would be entitled to any portion of his/her estate upon his/her death under any will or codicil thereto then existing or under the Intestate Succession Act as it provided at that time, and (iii) they were not a physician attending him/her, nor an employee of an attending physician, nor an employee of a health facility in which he/she was a patient, nor an employee of a nursing home or any group-care home in which he/she resided, and (iv) they did not have a claim against him/her. I further certify that I am satisfied as to the genuineness and due execution of the instrument.

This the 15th day of March, 2006.

John Allen Smith
NOTARY PUBLIC
Orange County, NC

John Allen Smith
Notary Public
My commission expires: April 15, 2008

4.9 Motor Vehicle Title Documents

Notaries frequently acknowledge the execution of applications to transfer motor vehicle titles, as well as applications for new titles. Only the applicant should complete the forms, except for the certificate. Notaries should adhere to certain precautions when taking an acknowledgment of a title document due to its special nature, as discussed in section 5.5. When notarizing motor vehicle title documents, notaries should be aware of the following:

- The forms depicted here do not indicate where the notary's typed or printed name should appear. To comply with the Notary Act, the notary should include it in an appropriate place, such as on the same line as the notary's signature.
- On some forms there are no spaces for the names of the county and state in which the notarization occurred. If the form does not require it, this information is not necessary for the form's acceptance by the Division of Motor Vehicles (DMV).
- Motor vehicle title forms require acknowledgments; proofs are not acceptable.
- Some title forms include jurats, while others do not. If a jurat is included, the applicant must give an oath or affirmation.
- Spelling or similar errors may cause the form to be rejected.
- All blanks for names and addresses, odometer readings, and similar information should be filled in by the applicant *before* the acknowledgment is taken.
- If an error was made in the first or middle name (for example, because of a misspelling or use of a nickname), the name should not be erased or covered with white out. A line should be drawn through the name and a correction entered above it or to its side.
- An error in a last name must be corrected with an affidavit; any alteration in the last name makes the assignment void. Affidavits from the seller, buyer, and lienholder and a new assignment without alterations will be required.
- The DMV requires full printed names and signatures, just as they appear on the reverse side of the title, for the subjects of the form. A person's middle name must be included; a woman should provide her given name, previous surname or middle name, and last name.
- Titles such as "Mr.," "Mrs.," "Ms.," "Dr.," and so forth should not be used.
- A person making a false statement under oath with regard to motor vehicle title documents is guilty of a Class I felony.[47]

Over the years the DMV has produced several different versions of the title form, many of which are still in circulation. Several follow as examples.

---

47. G.S. 20-112.

4.9.1 MVR-191 Form

Form MVR-191 has a certificate of title on one side and sections for assignments and an application for a new certificate of title on the other. The form's certificate arrangement can be problematic for notaries, easily leading to errors which can result in violation of the Notary Act or invalidate the form as required by the DMV. The Department of the Secretary of State recommends that notaries refer applicants using this form to the DMV for notarization.

The following depicts information required for Part A, the First Re-assignment of Title by Registered Owner.

Federal and State law requires that you state the mileage in connection with the transfer of ownership. Failure to complete or providing a false statement may result in fines and/or imprisonment.

A FIRST RE-ASSIGNMENT OF TITLE BY REGISTERED OWNER

The undersigned hereby certifies that the vehicle described in this title has been transferred to the following printed name and address:

Name of Buyer: **A**

Address of Buyer: **B**

I, seller(s) certify to the best of my knowledge that the odometer reading is the actual mileage of the vehicle unless one of the following statements is checked.

C
ODOMETER READING (No tenths)

☐ 1. The mileage stated is in excess of its mechanical limits.
☐ 2. The odometer reading is not the actual mileage.
WARNING   ODOMETER DISCREPANCY

To my knowledge the vehicle described herein:
Yes ☐ No ☐ Has been involved in a collision or other occurrence to the extent that the cost to repair exceeds 25% of fair market value.
D
Yes ☐ No ☐ Has been a flood vehicle.
Yes ☐ No ☐ Has been a reconstructed or a salvage vehicle.

Date vehicle delivered to purchaser **E**

Seller(s) Signature **F**
Seller(s) Hand Printed Name **G**
Notary Public **H**
Acknowledged before me this **I** day of **J** , 20 **K**
My Commission expires **L** (SEAL)
Buyer(s) Signature **M**
Buyer(s) Hand Printed Name **N**

B FIRST RE-ASSIGNMENT OF TITLE BY DEALER

A. Full typed or printed name of buyer
B. Buyer's street address and city or town
C. Odometer reading on date reassignment of title is executed
D. Yes and no questions concerning condition of vehicle that must be answered
E. Date vehicle delivered to buyer (usually date of title reassignment)
F. Seller's full signature

G. Seller's full hand-printed name
H. Notary's signature, typed or printed name, and seal
I. Date notary takes certification
J. Month notary takes certification
K. Year notary takes certification
L. Date notary's commission expires
M. Buyer's full signature
N. Buyer's full hand-printed name

The following is a sample of a completed First Re-assignment of Title by Registered Owner. The notary's certificate is for the seller's signature.

Federal and State law requires that you state the mileage in connection with the transfer of ownership. Failure to complete or providing a false statement may result in fines and/or imprisonment.

A FIRST RE-ASSIGNMENT OF TITLE BY REGISTERED OWNER

The undersigned hereby certifies that the vehicle described in this title has been transferred to the following printed name and address:

Name of Buyer: **Don's Used Cars**

Address of Buyer: **305 Monterrey, Fayetteville**

I, seller(s) certify to the best of my knowledge that the odometer reading is the actual mileage of the vehicle unless one of the following statements is checked.

33,456
ODOMETER READING (No tenths)

☐ 1. The mileage stated is in excess of its mechanical limits.
☐ 2. The odometer reading is not the actual mileage.
WARNING   ODOMETER DISCREPANCY

To my knowledge the vehicle described herein:
Yes ☐ No ☑ Has been involved in a collision or other occurrence to the extent that the cost to repair exceeds 25% of fair market value.
Yes ☐ No ☑ Has been a flood vehicle.
Yes ☐ No ☑ Has been a reconstructed or a salvage vehicle.

Date vehicle delivered to purchaser **12-15-05**

Seller(s) Signature *Kelly Brandon Simpson*
Seller(s) Hand Printed Name **Kelly Brandon Simpson**
Notary Public *Barbara J. Jones* **Barbara J. Jones**
Acknowledged before me this **15**th day of **December** , 20 **05**
My Commission expires **3-15-2008** (SEAL)
Buyer(s) Signature *Don's Used Cars, by Tom Smith*
Buyer(s) Hand Printed Name **Don's Used Cars by Tom Smith**

B FIRST RE-ASSIGNMENT OF TITLE BY DEALER

The following depicts information required for Part B, the First Re-assignment of Title by Dealer.

A. Full typed or printed name of buyer
B. Buyer's street address and city or town
C. Odometer reading on date reassignment of title is executed
D. Yes and no questions concerning condition of vehicle that must be answered
E. Date vehicle delivered to purchaser (usually date of title reassignment)
F. Full typed or printed name of dealer
G. Dealer's certificate number
H. Full signature of dealer's agent (omission of this item will cause title application to be rejected)

I. Full hand-printed name of agent signing for dealership
J. Notary's signature, typed or printed name, and seal
K. Date notary takes certification
L. Month notary takes certification
M. Year notary takes certification
N. Date notary's commission expires
O. Buyer's full signature
P. Buyer's full hand-printed name

The following is a sample of a completed First Re-assignment of Title by Dealer. The notary's certificate is for the signature of the dealer's representative.

The following depicts information required for Part C, the Purchaser's Application for New Certificate of Title.

A. Purchaser's driver's license number	N. Lienholder's city
B. Full typed or printed name of purchaser as shown on driver's license	O. Lienholder's state
	P. Lienholder's zip code
C. Purchaser's street address	Q. Full typed or printed name of insurance company issuing policy that insures vehicle
D. Purchaser's city or town	
E. Purchaser's state (which should be only North Carolina)	R. Insurance policy number
	S. Odometer reading on date application signed
F. Purchaser's zip code	
G. Purchaser's tax county	T. Purchaser's full signature
H. Purchaser's mailing address if different from residence or business address	U. Date notary takes certification
	V. Month notary takes certification
I. Date first lien created	W. Year notary takes certification
J. Account number provided by lienholder	X. Date notary's commission expires
K. Lienholder's identification number	Y. Notary's signature, typed or printed name, and seal
L. Holder of first lien	
M. Lienholder's address	

The following is a sample of a completed Purchaser's Application for New Certificate of Title.

C | PURCHASER S APPLICATION FOR NEW CERTIFICATE OF TITLE

The undersigned purchaser of the vehicle described on the face of this certificate, hereby makes application for a new certificate of title and certifies that said vehicle is subject to the following named liens and none other and that the information contained herein is true and accurate to my best knowledge and belief.

OWNER(S)
Owner 1 DL# **12534**   **Jennifer Hatch Boone**
                                               Full Legal name of Owner (First, Middle, Last, Suffix) or Company

Owner 2 DL# _____   _____
                                               Full Legal name of Owner (First, Middle, Last, Suffix) or Company

Residence Address **205 Forest Drive**

City **Wendell**   State **NC**   Zip Code **27591**   Tax County **Wake County**

Mail Address (if different from above) _____

FIRST LIEN
Date of Lien **1/6/2006** Account # **458455** Lienholder ID **14545**

SECOND LIEN
Date of Lien _____ Account # _____ Lienholder ID _____

Lienholder Name **First Family Bank**
Address **1100 New Bern Ave**
City **Raleigh** State **NC** Zip Code **27697**

Lienholder Name _____
Address _____
City _____ State _____ Zip Code _____

I certify for the motor vehicle described herein that I have financial responsibility as required by law.

Insurance Company Authorized in NC **State One Insurance**   Policy Number **458455555**

ODOMETER READING
33,973

Signature of Owner(s) *Jennifer Hatch Boone*

Acknowledged before me this **6th** day of **January**, 20 **06**   My commission expires **12-7-2008**

Notary Public *Mary Ann Ray*   **Mary Ann Ray**   (SEAL)

NOTE: RETAIL PURCHASER MUST APPLY FOR NEW TITLE WITHIN 28 DAYS AFTER PURCHASE OR PAY STATUTORY PENALTY. ALTERATION OR ERASURES WILL VOID THIS TITLE.

4.9.2 Reassignment of Title Form

The following version of the reassignment of title form continues in circulation.

Federal and State law requires that you state the mileage in connection with the transfer of ownership. Failure to complete or providing a false statement may result in fines and/or imprisonment.

A | **ASSIGNMENT OF TITLE BY REGISTERED OWNER**

The undersigned hereby certifies that the vehicle described in this title has been transferred to the following printed name and address.

"I certify to the best of my knowledge that the odometer reading is: _____ (NO TENTHS) and reflects the actual mileage of this vehicle unless one of the following statements is checked."

☐ 1. The mileage stated is in excess of its mechanical limits.
☐ 2. The odometer reading is not the actual mileage   **WARNING — ODOMETER DISCREPANCY**

| DATE VEHICLE DELIVERED TO PURCHASER |

To my knowledge the vehicle described herein
Yes ☐ No ☐ Has been involved in a collision or other occurrence to the extent that the cost to repair exceeds 25% of fair market retail value.
Yes ☐ No ☐ Has been a flood vehicle, a reconstructed vehicle or a salvage vehicle.

Hand Printed Name and
Signature(s) of Seller(s)_____

Acknowledged before me this _____ day of _____, _____ County _____ State _____

Notary Public _____   My Commission expires the _____ day of _____. _____

"I am aware of the above odometer certification and damage disclosure made by the seller."   (SEAL)

Hand Printed Name and
Signature(s) of Buyer(s)_____

B | **FIRST RE-ASSIGNMENT OF TITLE BY DEALER**

The undersigned hereby certifies that the vehicle described in this title has been transferred to the following printed name and address.

"I certify to the best of my knowledge that the odometer reading is: _____ (NO TENTHS) and reflects the actual mileage of this vehicle unless one of the following statements is checked."

☐ 1. The mileage stated is in excess of its mechanical limits.
☐ 2. The odometer reading is not the actual mileage   **WARNING — ODOMETER DISCREPANCY**

| DATE VEHICLE DELIVERED TO PURCHASER |

To my knowledge the vehicle described herein
Yes ☐ No ☐ Has been involved in a collision or other occurrence to the extent that the cost to repair exceeds 25% of fair market retail value.
Yes ☐ No ☐ Has been a flood vehicle, a reconstructed vehicle or a salvage vehicle.

Hand Printed Name and
Signature(s) of dealer or agent _____ Dealer's No. _____

Printed Firm Name _____

Acknowledged before me this _____ day of _____, _____ County _____ State _____

Notary Public _____   My Commission expires the _____ day of _____. _____

"I am aware of the above odometer certification and damage disclosure made by the seller."   (SEAL)

Hand Printed Name and
Signature(s) of Buyer(s) _____

C | **PURCHASER'S APPLICATION FOR NEW CERTIFICATE OF TITLE**

THE UNDERSIGNED, PURCHASER OF THE VEHICLE DESCRIBED ON THE FACE OF THIS CERTIFICATE, HEREBY MAKES APPLICATION FOR A NEW CERTIFICATE OF TITLE AND CERTIFIES THAT SAID VEHICLE IS SUBJECT TO THE FOLLOWING NAMED LIENS AND NONE OTHER, AND THAT THE INFORMATION CONTAINED HEREIN IS TRUE AND ACCURATE TO MY BEST KNOWLEDGE AND BELIEF.

FIRST LIEN		SECOND LIEN	
DATE _____	ACCOUNT # _____	DATE _____	ACCOUNT # _____
LIENHOLDER ID#	LIENHOLDER NAME	LIENHOLDER ID#	LIENHOLDER NAME
ADDRESS		ADDRESS	
CITY	STATE	ZIP CODE	CITY	STATE	ZIP CODE

DISCLOSURE SECTION

All motor vehicle records maintained by the North Carolina Division of Motor Vehicles will remain closed for marketing and solicitation unless the block below is checked.

☐ I (We) would like the personal information contained in this application **to be available for disclosure.**

I CERTIFY FOR THE MOTOR VEHICLE DESCRIBED ON THIS TITLE THAT I HAVE FINANCIAL RESPONSIBILITY AS REQUIRED BY LAW

Print or type full name of Insurance company authorized in N.C.-not agency or group   Policy number-If policy not issued, name of agency binding coverage

SIGNATURE OF PURCHASER(S) | Plate to be transferred | Odometer Reading (No Tenths) |

FIRST NAME   MIDDLE NAME   LAST NAME

PRINT IN INK OR TYPE NAME EXACTLY AS IT APPEARS ABOVE IN SIGNATURE | D. L. Number Owner 1 | D. L. Number Owner 2 |

ACKNOWLEDGED BEFORE ME

RESIDENCE ADDRESS   THIS _____ DAY OF _____

POST OFFICE   COUNTY OF RESIDENCE   ZIP CODE   MY COMMISSION EXPIRES _____

MAILING ADDRESS IF DIFFERENT FROM ABOVE   SIGNATURE OF NOTARY PUBLIC IN INK _____ (SEAL)

NOTE: RETAIL PURCHASER MUST APPLY FOR NEW TITLE WITHIN 28 DAYS AFTER PURCHASE OR PAY STATUTORY PENALTY. ALTERATIONS OR ERASURES WILL VOID THIS TITLE.

The following depicts information required for Part A, the Assignment of Title by Registered Owner.

A. Full typed or printed name of purchaser
B. Purchaser's street address and city or town
C. Odometer reading on date assignment of title is executed
D. Date vehicle delivered to purchaser (usually date of title assignment)
E. Yes and no questions concerning condition of vehicle that must be answered
F. Seller's full hand-printed name
G. Seller's full signature
H. Date notary takes certification
I. Month notary takes certification

J. Year notary takes certification
K. County in which assignment executed
L. State in which assignment executed
M. Notary's signature, typed or printed name, and seal
N. Date notary's commission expires
O. Month and year notary's commission expires
P. Buyer's full hand-printed name
Q. Buyer's full signature

The following is an example of a completed Assignment of Title by Registered Owner for the form depicted above. The certificate is for the seller's signature.

The following depicts information required for Part B, the First Re-assignment of Title by Dealer.

A. Full typed or printed name of purchaser

B. Purchaser's street address and city or town

C. Odometer reading on date reassignment of title is executed

D. Date vehicle delivered to purchaser (usually date of title reassignment)

E. Yes and no questions concerning condition of vehicle that must be answered

F. Full hand-printed name of agent signing for dealership

G. Full signature of dealer's agent (omission of this item will cause title application to be rejected)

H. Dealer's certificate number

I. Full typed or printed name of dealer

J. Date notary takes certification

K. Month and year notary takes certification

L. County in which reassignment executed

M. State in which reassignment executed

N. Notary's signature, typed or printed name, and seal

O. Date notary's commission expires

P. Month and year notary's commission expires

Q. Buyer's full hand-printed name

R. Buyer's full signature

The following is an example of a completed First Re-assignment of Title by Dealer for the form depicted above. The certificate is for the signature of the dealer's representative.

The following depicts information required for Part C, the Purchaser's Application for New Certificate of Title.

PURCHASER'S APPLICATION FOR NEW CERTIFICATE OF TITLE

THE UNDERSIGNED, PURCHASER OF THE VEHICLE DESCRIBED ON THE FACE OF THIS CERTIFICATE, HEREBY MAKES APPLICATION FOR A NEW CERTIFICATE OF TITLE AND CERTIFIES THAT SAID VEHICLE IS SUBJECT TO THE FOLLOWING NAMED LIENS AND NONE OTHER, AND THAT THE INFORMATION CONTAINED HEREIN IS TRUE AND ACCURATE TO MY BEST KNOWLEDGE AND BELIEF.

FIRST LIEN

DATE **A**   ACCOUNT # **B**

C   **D**

LIENHOLDER ID#   LIENHOLDER NAME
E

ADDRESS
F   **G**   **H**

CITY   STATE   ZIP CODE

SECOND LIEN

DATE _____   ACCOUNT # _____

LIENHOLDER ID#   LIENHOLDER NAME

ADDRESS

CITY   STATE   ZIP CODE

DISCLOSURE SECTION

All motor vehicle records maintained by the North Carolina Division of Motor Vehicles will remain closed for marketing and solicitation unless the block below is checked.

☐ I (We) would like the personal information contained in this application **to be available for disclosure.**

I

I CERTIFY FOR THE MOTOR VEHICLE DESCRIBED ON THIS TITLE THAT I HAVE FINANCIAL RESPONSIBILITY AS REQUIRED BY LAW

J   **K**

Print or type full name of insurance company authorized in N.C.-not agency or group   Policy number-If policy not issued, name of agency binding coverage

SIGNATURE OF PURCHASER(S)

L

FIRST NAME   MIDDLE NAME   LAST NAME

M

PRINT IN INK OR TYPE NAME EXACTLY AS IT APPEARS ABOVE IN SIGNATURE

N

RESIDENCE ADDRESS

O   **P**   **Q**

POST OFFICE   COUNTY OF RESIDENCE   ZIP CODE

R

MAILING ADDRESS IF DIFFERENT FROM ABOVE

S Plate to be transferred   **T** Odometer Reading (No Tenths)

U

D. L. Number Owner 1   D. L. Number Owner 2

ACKNOWLEDGED BEFORE ME

THIS **V** _____ DAY OF **W** _____

MY COMMISSION EXPIRES **X** _____

Y _____ (SEAL)

SIGNATURE OF NOTARY PUBLIC IN INK

NOTE: RETAIL PURCHASER MUST APPLY FOR NEW TITLE WITHIN 28 DAYS AFTER PURCHASE OR PAY STATUTORY PENALTY. ALTERATIONS OR ERASURES WILL VOID THIS TITLE.

A. Date first lien created

B. Account number provided by lienholder

C. Lienholder's identification number

D. Holder of first lien

E. Lienholder's address

F. Lienholder's city

G. Lienholder's state

H. Lienholder's zip code

I. Disclosure Section

J. Full typed or printed name of insurance company issuing policy that insures vehicle

K. Insurance policy number

L. Purchaser's full signature

M. Full typed or printed name of purchaser

N. Purchaser's street address, city, and state

O. Purchaser's post office box

P. Purchaser's county of residence

Q. Purchaser's zip code

R. Purchaser's mailing address if different from residence or business address

S. Plate to be transferred

T. Odometer reading on date application signed

U. Purchaser's driver's license number

V. Date notary takes certification

W. Month and year notary takes certification

X. Date notary's commission expires

Y. Notary's signature, typed or printed name, and seal

The following is an example of a completed Purchaser's Application for New Certificate of Title for the form depicted above.

PURCHASER'S APPLICATION FOR NEW CERTIFICATE OF TITLE

THE UNDERSIGNED, PURCHASER OF THE VEHICLE DESCRIBED ON THE FACE OF THIS CERTIFICATE, HEREBY MAKES APPLICATION FOR A NEW CERTIFICATE OF TITLE AND CERTIFIES THAT SAID VEHICLE IS SUBJECT TO THE FOLLOWING NAMED LIENS AND NONE OTHER, AND THAT THE INFORMATION CONTAINED HEREIN IS TRUE AND ACCURATE TO MY BEST KNOWLEDGE AND BELIEF.

FIRST LIEN	SECOND LIEN
DATE _____ ACCOUNT # _____	DATE _____ ACCOUNT # _____
LIENHOLDER ID# _____ LIENHOLDER NAME _____	LIENHOLDER ID# _____ LIENHOLDER NAME _____
ADDRESS _____	ADDRESS _____
CITY _____ STATE _____ ZIP CODE _____	CITY _____ STATE _____ ZIP CODE _____

DISCLOSURE SECTION

All motor vehicle records maintained by the North Carolina Division of Motor Vehicles will remain closed for marketing and solicitation unless the block below is checked.

☐ I (We) would like the personal information contained in this application **to be available for disclosure.**

I CERTIFY FOR THE MOTOR VEHICLE DESCRIBED ON THIS TITLE THAT I HAVE FINANCIAL RESPONSIBILITY AS REQUIRED BY LAW

Wide State Insurance Company   **1066-1453-ONOC**

Print or type full name of Insurance company authorized in N.C.-not agency, or group   Policy number-if policy not issued, name of agency binding coverage

SIGNATURE OF PURCHASER(S)   *Charles Taylor Smith*

Plate to be transferred   Odometer Reading (No Tenths) **53,102**

| FIRST NAME **Charles** | MIDDLE NAME **Taylor** | LAST NAME **Smith** | | **NC5555** |

PRINT IN INK OR TYPE NAME EXACTLY AS IT APPEARS ABOVE IN SIGNATURE   D. L. Number Owner 1   D. L. Number Owner 2

10 Spring Street   New Bern, NC

RESIDENCE ADDRESS

ACKNOWLEDGED BEFORE ME THIS **20th** DAY OF **May** **2005**

POST OFFICE **Craven**   COUNTY OF RESIDENCE   ZIP CODE **27220**

MY COMMISSION EXPIRES **12-7-2008**

MAILING ADDRESS IF DIFFERENT FROM ABOVE   *Mary Carolyn Smith* **Mary Carolyn Smith** (SEAL)

SIGNATURE OF NOTARY PUBLIC IN INK

NOTE: RETAIL PURCHASER MUST APPLY FOR NEW TITLE WITHIN 28 DAYS AFTER PURCHASE OR PAY STATUTORY PENALTY. ALTERATIONS OR ERASURES WILL VOID THIS TITLE.

4.9.3 Title Certificate Form

The following title certificate has been in use for several years. It consists of two sections: Part A for the assignment of title by the current registered owner, and Part B for the reassignment of title by a registered dealer. In Part A the notary is taking the acknowledgment of the seller only. The purchaser's application for a new title must be made on the MVR-1 form, depicted later in this chapter.

The following depicts information required for Part A, the Assignment of Title by Registered Owner.

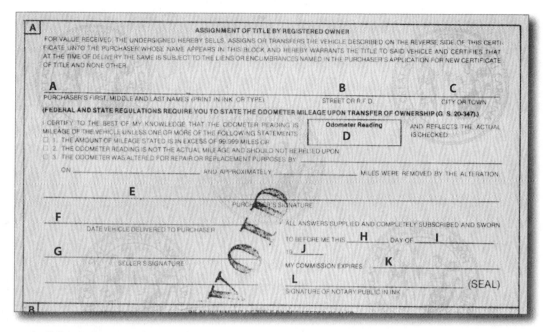

A. Full typed or printed name of purchaser

B. Purchaser's street address

C. Purchaser's city or town

D. Odometer reading on date assignment of title is executed

E. Purchaser's full signature

F. Date vehicle delivered to purchaser (usually date of title assignment)

G. Seller's full signature

H. Date notary takes certification

I. Month notary takes certification

J. Year notary takes certification

K. Month, date, and year notary's commission expires

L. Notary's signature, typed or printed name, and seal

The following depicts information required for Part B, the Re-assignment of Title by Registered Dealer.

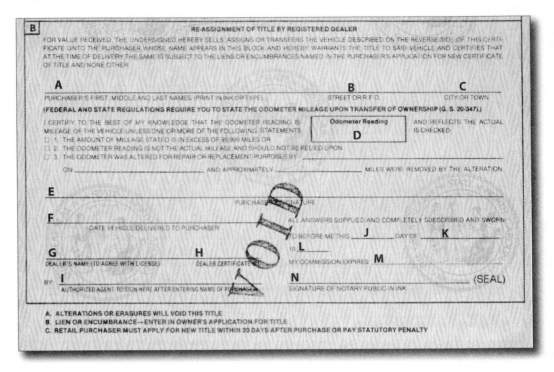

A. Full typed or printed name of purchaser

B. Purchaser's street address

C. Purchaser's city or town

D. Odometer reading on date reassignment of title is executed

E. Purchaser's full signature

F. Date vehicle delivered to purchaser

G. Full typed or printed name of dealer

H. Dealer's certificate number

I. Full signature of dealer's agent (omission of this item will cause title application to be rejected)

J. Date notary takes certification

K. Month notary takes certification

L. Year notary takes certification

M. Month, date, and year notary's commission expires

N. Notary's signature, typed or printed name, and seal

The following is an example of completed parts A and B of the form described above.

A   ASSIGNMENT OF TITLE BY REGISTERED OWNER

FOR VALUE RECEIVED, THE UNDERSIGNED HEREBY SELLS, ASSIGNS OR TRANSFERS THE VEHICLE DESCRIBED ON THE REVERSE SIDE OF THIS CERTI-
FICATE UNTO THE PURCHASER WHOSE NAME APPEARS IN THIS BLOCK AND HEREBY WARRANTS THE TITLE TO SAID VEHICLE AND CERTIFIES THAT
AT THE TIME OF DELIVERY THE SAME IS SUBJECT TO THE LIENS OR ENCUMBRANCES NAMED IN THE PURCHASER'S APPLICATION FOR NEW CERTIFICATE
OF TITLE AND NONE OTHER.

Hawkins Motor Company   **2 Lions Blvd**   **Charlotte**

PURCHASER'S FIRST, MIDDLE AND LAST NAMES (PRINT IN INK OR TYPE)   STREET OR R.F.D.   CITY OR TOWN

(FEDERAL AND STATE REGULATIONS REQUIRE YOU TO STATE THE ODOMETER MILEAGE UPON TRANSFER OF OWNERSHIP (G. S. 20-347.)

I CERTIFY TO THE BEST OF MY KNOWLEDGE THAT THE ODOMETER READING IS   **Odometer Reading**   AND REFLECTS THE ACTUAL
MILEAGE OF THE VEHICLE UNLESS ONE OR MORE OF THE FOLLOWING STATEMENTS   **88049**   IS CHECKED:
☐ 1. THE AMOUNT OF MILEAGE STATED IS IN EXCESS OF 99,999 MILES OR
☐ 2. THE ODOMETER READING IS NOT THE ACTUAL MILEAGE AND SHOULD NOT BE RELIED UPON
☐ 3. THE ODOMETER WAS ALTERED FOR REPAIR OR REPLACEMENT PURPOSES BY _____

ON _____ AND APPROXIMATELY _____ MILES WERE REMOVED BY THE ALTERATION.

Hawkins Motor Company   *Jennifer Smith*

PURCHASER'S SIGNATURE

5/19/2005

DATE VEHICLE DELIVERED TO PURCHASER   ALL ANSWERS SUPPLIED AND COMPLETELY SUBSCRIBED AND SWORN

Alex Wilder Stewart   TO BEFORE ME THIS **19th** DAY OF **May**

SELLER'S SIGNATURE   **2005**

MY COMMISSION EXPIRES   **February 5, 2008**

Allison Sprague   **Allison Sprague**   (SEAL)

SIGNATURE OF NOTARY PUBLIC IN INK

B   RE-ASSIGNMENT OF TITLE BY REGISTERED DEALER

FOR VALUE RECEIVED, THE UNDERSIGNED HEREBY SELLS, ASSIGNS OR TRANSFERS THE VEHICLE DESCRIBED ON THE REVERSE SIDE OF THIS CERTI-
FICATE UNTO THE PURCHASER WHOSE NAME APPEARS IN THIS BLOCK AND HEREBY WARRANTS THE TITLE TO SAID VEHICLE AND CERTIFIES THAT
AT THE TIME OF DELIVERY THE SAME IS SUBJECT TO THE LIENS OR ENCUMBRANCES NAMED IN THE PURCHASER'S APPLICATION FOR NEW CERTIFICATE
OF TITLE AND NONE OTHER.

David Rose French   **4 Talmage Court**   **Charlotte**

PURCHASER'S FIRST, MIDDLE AND LAST NAMES (PRINT IN INK OR TYPE)   STREET OR R.F.D.   CITY OR TOWN

(FEDERAL AND STATE REGULATIONS REQUIRE YOU TO STATE THE ODOMETER MILEAGE UPON TRANSFER OF OWNERSHIP (G.S. 20-347.)

I CERTIFY TO THE BEST OF MY KNOWLEDGE THAT THE ODOMETER READING IS   **Odometer Reading**   AND REFLECTS THE ACTUAL
MILEAGE OF THE VEHICLE UNLESS ONE OR MORE OF THE FOLLOWING STATEMENTS   **88049**   IS CHECKED:
☐ 1. THE AMOUNT OF MILEAGE STATED IS IN EXCESS OF 99,999 MILES OR
☐ 2. THE ODOMETER READING IS NOT THE ACTUAL MILEAGE AND SHOULD NOT BE RELIED UPON
☐ 3. THE ODOMETER WAS ALTERED FOR REPAIR OR REPLACEMENT PURPOSES BY _____

ON _____ AND APPROXIMATELY _____ MILES WERE REMOVED BY THE ALTERATION.

David Rose French

PURCHASER'S SIGNATURE

5-20-2005

DATE VEHICLE DELIVERED TO PURCHASER   ALL ANSWERS SUPPLIED AND COMPLETELY SUBSCRIBED AND SWORN

Hawkins Motor Company 8116   TO BEFORE ME THIS **20th** DAY OF **May**

DEALER'S NAME (TO AGREE WITH LICENSE)   DEALER CERTIFICATE #   **2005**

MY COMMISSION EXPIRES   **12-7-2008**

BY *Lisa Smith Stephens*   *Mary Tass Stewart*   **Mary Tass Stewart**   (SEAL)

AUTHORIZED AGENT TO SIGN HERE AFTER ENTERING NAME OF PURCHASER   SIGNATURE OF NOTARY PUBLIC IN INK

A. ALTERATIONS OR ERASURES WILL VOID THIS TITLE
B. LIEN OR ENCUMBRANCE—ENTER IN OWNER'S APPLICATION FOR TITLE
C. RETAIL PURCHASER MUST APPLY FOR NEW TITLE WITHIN 20 DAYS AFTER PURCHASE OR PAY STATUTORY PENALTY

4.9.4 MVR-1 Form

This is the most recent version of the title application form, MVR-1, which must be used when the former owner has assigned a title by means of a DMV certificate of title form that does not contain a section for the purchaser to apply for a new certificate of title.

The following is an example of a completed acknowledgment certificate of the MVR-1 form:

4.10 Notarial Components of Electronic Documents

An electronic notary creates a record of an electronic notarial act and attaches it to, or logically associates it with, the electronic document. Each of the following elements, some of which are intended to clarify that the act was electronically performed, must be immediately perceptible and reproducible in the electronic record:[48]

- The notary's name, state, and county of commissioning exactly as they are stated on the notary's commission
- The words "Electronic Notary Public"
- The words "State of North Carolina"
- The notary's commission expiration date
- The notary's electronic signature
- An appropriate certificate for the notarial act

This required information includes the elements that constitute the notary's electronic seal.[49]

---

48. G.S. 10B-117.
49. G.S. 10B-101(5).

CHAPTER 5

COMMON NOTARIAL SETTINGS

Notaries who are not attorneys are prohibited from "assist[ing] another person in drafting, completing, selecting, or understanding a record or transaction requiring a notarial act;"[1] doing so constitutes the unauthorized practice of law. Although nonattorney notaries do not draft legal instruments or give legal advice about the content of those instruments, they must ensure that the certificates they complete comply with required and sound notarial practices. The following discussion about common types of settings encountered by notaries is intended to acquaint notaries with the nature of the most common documents they may be asked to notarize—not to aid notaries in engaging in the unlawful practice of law.

5.1 Affidavits, Verifications, and Depositions

Affidavits, verifications, and depositions are commonly encountered in court proceedings. A notary must take an oath or affirmation before completing certificates for these documents.

5.1.1 Affidavits
An *affidavit* is a written statement about certain facts and affirmed as true by oath or affirmation. Unlike depositions, which are part of a litigation discovery process, affidavits are

---

1. N.C. GEN. STAT. § 10B-20(k) (hereinafter G.S.).

voluntary statements used in a variety of government and business affairs—for example, as evidence of a property title, animal pedigree, an individual's age, or the financial status of a loan applicant.

A North Carolina notary public acting within North Carolina may notarize affidavits except when the law prescribes another official before whom an affidavit must be sworn in a particular context. For example, the law provides that only the clerk of superior court can take an insolvent debtor's affidavit for assignment of his or her estate for the benefit of creditors.[2] In addition, a notary may not take his or her own affidavit, since a notary may not administer an oath to him- or herself.

Federal laws also allow affidavits to be used in many ways. Because North Carolina notaries acting within North Carolina may administer oaths under federal law,[3] they may also take affidavits under federal law (except for specific affidavits that must be taken by another designated official).

Preparing an affidavit sufficient to accomplish a desired result is the responsibility of the party and the party's attorney. The notary's responsibility is to adhere to the requirements of the notarial act, including verifying the affiant's identity and ensuring that the affiant swears to or affirms the truthfulness of the statements in the affidavit. As with all notarial acts, the notary must also properly complete the certificate. A typical affidavit includes the following components:

- *Caption.* An affidavit for a legal proceeding should include a caption that recites the county and state in which the action is pending, the parties' names, the court's name, and the label "Affidavit." Other types of affidavits should include a title briefly describing the nature of the matter and naming the county and state in which the affidavit was given.
- *Preamble.* The preamble follows the caption and is simply a statement that the named person appeared before the notary, was duly sworn, and made the affidavit. Although not essential to an affidavit's validity, the preamble is usually included for introductory purposes.
- *Allegations.* The statements of the affiant follow the preamble, usually in numbered paragraphs, each paragraph containing only one allegation. The first allegation should always state the affiant's relationship to the action or to the parties involved.
- *Affiant's signature.* Although the absence of the affiant's signature does not technically invalidate an affidavit,[4] the affiant should sign his or her name below the allegations. Omission of a signature raises doubts about the affidavit's validity and may invalidate it in other states. In any event, a notary should not knowingly notarize a document without the subject's signature.
- *Jurat.* The jurat, or notary's certificate that the affidavit was subscribed and sworn to (or affirmed) at a specified time and place, appears after the affiant's signature. The jurat should be attested by a notary in the usual manner.

---

2. G.S. 23-13.
3. 5 U.S.C. § 2903(c)(2).
4. Alford v. McCormac, 90 N.C. 151, 153 (1884).

5.1.2 Verification of Pleadings

In some kinds of lawsuits—such as divorce,[5] habeas corpus,[6] or certain suits by shareholders or members of a corporation or unincorporated association[7]—the parties or their attorneys "verify" the allegations they file with the court by executing an affidavit of verification according to Rule 11 of the North Carolina Rules of Civil Procedure. The content of the affidavit varies according to the type of lawsuit, and the party seeking the affidavit and his or her attorney are responsible for preparing it correctly. The notary's responsibilities are to administer an oath or affirmation and to complete the jurat, or certification, correctly.

5.1.3 Depositions

A *deposition* commonly is an oral examination of a witness or of a party to a transaction, and it may be taken by agreement or compelled by a subpoena. The deposition is taken under oath or affirmation and memorialized with a transcript. A notary or other qualified official certifies that the deponent gave an oath or affirmation as to the truth of the deposition. Depositions also can be given as responses to written questions. The written responses must be given under oath or affirmation, which is reflected by a jurat. Lawsuits also commonly involve interrogatories, which are completed by a party and signed without need for notarization.

5.2 Real Estate Documents

Real estate transactions usually are important events in the lives of those involved. The purchase or sale of real estate is likely to be a substantial financial and emotional investment. In commercial transactions the purchase, sale, or financing of real estate can have a significant impact on a business and its affairs.

The event at which real estate is transferred or a loan secured by real estate is consummated is called the *closing*. Legal professionals will handle the closing and are responsible for ensuring that the instruments are correctly completed and filed with the appropriate public offices and that other aspects of the closing are conducted properly. Notaries who take acknowledgments at a closing should contribute to an atmosphere of conscientiousness and solemnity by properly performing the notarization and completing the certificate correctly. The following discussion is intended to familiarize notaries with the basics of what occurs in a common real estate transaction.

North Carolina law requires real estate conveyances to be in writing and to be signed by the grantor.[8] For a conveyance to bind third parties, the instrument must be registered with the register of deeds in the county in which the real estate is located.[9] Most real estate instruments, including deeds and deeds of trust, cannot be registered unless the signatures have been acknowledged or proved.[10] Before registering instruments that require acknowledgments or proofs, registers of deeds verify that "execution of the instrument by one or more signers appears to have been proved or acknowledged before an officer

---

5. G.S. 50-8.
6. G.S. 17-7(5).
7. N.C. R. Civ. P. 23(b).
8. G.S. 22-2.
9. G.S. 47-18.
10. G.S. 47-17.

with the apparent authority to take proofs or acknowledgements, and the said proof or acknowledgement includes the officer's signature, commission expiration date, and official seal, if required."[11] A register will not accept an instrument requiring an acknowledgment or proof if the signature, expiration date, or seal is missing. But by law a register is not "required to verify or make inquiry concerning (i) the legal sufficiency of any proof or acknowledgement, (ii) the authority of any officer who took a proof or acknowledgement, or (iii) the legal sufficiency of any document presented for registration."[12] Therefore, the register's acceptance of an instrument for registration does not ensure that the instrument includes a valid acknowledgment or proof. If the acknowledgment or proof associated with an instrument contains an obvious defect, the instrument is treated under the law as if it were not registered.[13] Consequently, the instrument's legal enforceability may depend on the notary's careful attention to the requirements of the acknowledgment or proof.

The most common real estate instruments acknowledged by notaries include deeds, deeds of trust, and satisfaction instruments. There are many other types of real estate instruments for which acknowledgments or proofs are required or appropriate, and in each instance the notary should adhere to the limitations and requirements discussed in this guidebook.

A *deed* is an instrument of conveyance in which real estate owners, or *grantors*, convey property interests to others, or *grantees*. The most common type of deed is a *warranty deed*, which contains warranties about title and the grantors' obligation to defend it. Less common are *special warranty deeds*, which limit the grantors' warranties to defects arising because of, through, or under the grantors, and *quitclaim deeds*, which simply transfer the grantors' interest without any warranties. All deeds contain the names of the parties and the grantees' mailing address, words of conveyance, a description of the property being conveyed, the signatures of all grantors, and an acknowledgment or proof of each signature. Deeds commonly do not include the grantees' signatures.

Title to real estate may be held by an individual or by a legal entity such as a corporation. Property owned by a husband and wife together is usually owned in the form of *tenants by the entireties*, in which one spouse becomes sole owner upon the other's death, and neither spouse may convey or mortgage the property without the other's consent. A similar form of common ownership is *joint tenants with rights of survivorship*, in which a survivor becomes sole owner upon the other's death. With a *tenancy in common*, each of multiple owners has a full right of possession, but each has an interest that may be transferred separately.

A *deed of trust* and a *mortgage* are security instruments given by a property owner to a lender as security for repayment of a loan. Deeds of trust, which are more common than mortgages in North Carolina, involve three parties—the borrower, who conveys the property to a third party, known as the trustee, as security for the beneficiary, who is the lender or the lender's nominee. A mortgage involves only two parties—the mortgagor, or property owner and borrower, and the mortgagee, who is the lender or the lender's nominee. Both deeds of trust and mortgages give a lender the right to foreclose and sell the property if there is a default. Both types of documents will include the owner's name, the terms and conditions of the security instrument, a reference to the loan or obligation being secured, a description of the subject property, the signatures of all grantors, and an acknowledgment or proof of each signature.

---

11. G.S. 47-14(a).
12. G.S. 47-14(a).
13. McClure v. Crow, 196 N.C. 657, 146 S.E. 713 (1929).

Termination of a deed of trust or mortgage, which usually occurs when the loan has been paid from a sale or refinance, is reflected by a *satisfaction* instrument. A typical satisfaction instrument identifies the parties to the deed of trust or mortgage and the deed's or mortgage's recording data, and it will be signed and acknowledged by the secured lender or trustee. There are other methods by which a secured creditor can make a record of satisfaction, such as using a quitclaim deed or presenting endorsed instruments to the register.

While many real estate documents follow common forms, in some cases the instrument is a creature of a particular situation. In all cases, the precise contents of each real estate instrument are designed to accomplish a specific purpose. The basic certificate forms provided by the Notary Act are, by statute, sufficient for real estate instruments.[14] The statutes also provide a number of alternative certificate forms, including several for use by corporations and other entities, which legal practitioners may continue to use and notaries therefore may continue to encounter.

5.3 Estate Planning Documents

A number of important documents are prepared by attorneys to accomplish a person's objectives in connection with death and succession. A nonattorney notary may not prepare these documents for others or give advice about which documents will accomplish such objectives. Notarial certificates for estate planning documents are specialized and include information intended by the drafting attorneys to achieve certain presumptions of validity. Notaries who are not attorneys must rely on the drafting attorneys to ensure these certificates are sufficient for the purposes intended.

Most people appreciate the importance of the wills and other estate planning documents they sign. Attorneys will explain the significance of these documents and emphasize the need for careful attention to detail. Notaries must make certain that the certificates they sign are complete and accurate, including any information regarding the names of the principals and witnesses.

A *will* is someone's statement of intent about how property is to be distributed and other affairs handled after death. Because the testator, or the person making a will, will not be available to validate the will when it goes into effect, wills are subject to heightened validation requirements. The most common type of will in North Carolina is the "self-proved" will, in which prescribed oaths made by the testator and two witnesses are documented by a notary or other official. If this documentation is properly prepared and completed, the witnesses need not testify about the will's execution for the will to be admitted to probate.

A *trust* is an agreement by which the trust maker, called a grantor, gives instructions to a trustee concerning the receipt, management, and disposition of assets. A common form of trust is a revocable living trust, in which the grantor gives instructions about how assets are to be handled during the grantor's lifetime and upon death, but the grantor reserves the right to terminate or change the trust at any time. The trustee agreement is executed by the grantor and the trustee, whose signatures usually are acknowledged.

A *power of attorney* is a means for a person, the principal, to give someone else, an attorney-in-fact or agent, authority to make decisions for the principal. The statutory

---

14. G.S. 47-37.1(a).

short form of general power of attorney gives designated powers over property and financial affairs to the attorney-in-fact and includes a certificate form indicating an oath has been administered. A *durable power of attorney* gives the attorney-in-fact authority to make decisions for the principal in case of the principal's incapacity or mental incompetence. With a *limited* or *special power of attorney*, the principal gives the attorney-in-fact authority only over a particular matter, such as execution of documents in connection with the sale of specific real estate.

A *health care power of attorney* is used by a principal to authorize someone to make health care decisions for the principal if a doctor determines that the principal lacks sufficient understanding or capacity to make or communicate these decisions. The statutory form includes a prescribed notarial certificate including an oath to be made by the principal and two witnesses.[15]

A *living will*, which the statute calls A Declaration of a Desire for a Natural Death, is a direction to physicians authorizing the withholding or discontinuance of extraordinary means of postponing death artificially, and it may also authorize the withholding or discontinuance of artificial nutrition or hydration. The form of directive that complies with North Carolina law is specifically provided by the statutes and includes a prescribed certificate.[16]

5.4 Entities and Trusts

Notaries are likely to encounter documents executed by individuals in a representative capacity for legal entities such as corporations and associations, limited liability companies, partnerships and limited partnerships, and trusts. The following discussion is intended to familiarize notaries with these common entity forms and, as a general rule (possibly subject to exceptions in particular circumstances), those who have authority to sign on behalf of these entities.

A *corporation* is a traditional form of business entity favored because it allows the accumulation of capital through the sale of stocks and bonds and limits a *shareholder's* liability to the extent of the shareholder's contributions. To establish a corporation, an entity must complete the necessary steps for incorporation, including the filing of articles of incorporation, with a state governing authority, which in North Carolina is the Department of the Secretary of State.[17] The corporation's name must include the word "corporation," "incorporated," "company," or "limited" or the abbreviation "corp.," "inc.," "co.," or "ltd."[18] The corporation may enter into contracts, own property, and incur liabilities to the same extent as an individual.[19] North Carolina corporations must maintain a registered agent and an office in this state.[20] Fundamental decisions about corporate existence are made by the shareholders, who must meet at least annually.[21] Corporations usually have directors, to whom the shareholders delegate most manage-

---

15. G.S. 32A-25.
16. G.S. 90-321.
17. G.S. 55-2-03.
18. G.S. 55D-20(a)(1).
19. G.S. 55-3-02.
20. G.S. 55-5-01.
21. G.S. 55-7-01.

rial decisions.[22] The corporation's daily affairs are delegated to officers, who may or may not be directors, including a president or other presiding officer, treasurer or other chief financial officer, secretary, and in larger corporations, other officers, including vice presidents. For most significant transactions, officers are authorized to bind the corporation by a resolution of the board of directors. A corporation can be dissolved by a vote of the shareholders, by order of a court, or administratively if the company fails to comply with statutory requirements such as filing reports and paying fees.[23]

A *nonprofit corporation* also is created with the filing of articles of incorporation with the Department of the Secretary of State.[24] It, too, may enter into contracts, own property, and incur liabilities to the same extent as an individual,[25] and it generally has the same attributes and must meet the same requirements as a business corporation. It usually has *members* rather than shareholders who, like shareholders, are not personally liable for the corporation's obligations unless they so agree.[26] A nonprofit corporation has at least one director[27] and such officers as its bylaws provide.[28]

The *limited liability company* is a relatively new form of business entity, first recognized in North Carolina in 1993.[29] It is a popular type of business organization because it offers the liability protections of corporations, the tax advantages of partnerships, and ease and flexibility in formation. Limited liability companies are formed with articles of organization filed with the Department of the Secretary of State. A limited liability company's name must include the words "limited liability company," "ltd. liability co.," "limited liability co.," "ltd. liability company," or the abbreviation "L.L.C." or "LLC."[30] The company consists of *members* who automatically are considered to be *managers* unless the articles of organization provide otherwise.[31] As with other entities, a limited liability company can be dissolved by agreement of the members, by order of a court, or administratively if the company fails to comply with statutory requirements such as filing reports and paying fees.[32]

A *professional corporation* is one in which the stock must be held only by licensees of particular professional services, such as attorneys, accountants, surveyors, architects, physicians, dentists, or veterinarians.[33] The shareholders, directors, and officers of a professional corporation are not individually liable for errors of the other shareholders, directors, or officers.[34] A professional corporation's name must include the words or abbreviation "Professional Association," "P.A.," "Professional Corporation," or "P.C."[35]

A *partnership* is "an association of two or more persons to carry on as co-owners of a business for profit."[36] Unlike other forms of business entities, no formal agreement

---

22. G.S. 55-8-01.
23. G.S. 55-14-01, -02, -20, -30.
24. G.S. 55A-2-03.
25. G.S. 55A-3-02.
26. G.S. 55A-6-01, G.S. 55A-6-22.
27. G.S. 55A-8-03.
28. G.S. 55A-8-40.
29. 1993 N.C. Sess. Laws ch. 354; codified at G.S. Chapter 57C.
30. G.S. 55D-20(a)(2).
31. G.S. 57C-3-20(a).
32. G.S. 57C-3-6-01, -02, -03.
33. G.S. Chapter 55B.
34. G.S. 55B-9(b).
35. G.S. 55B-5.
36. G.S. 59-36(a).

or filing is required to form a partnership, but partnerships typically are governed by agreements that spell out the partners' rights and obligations, including partner liability for the partnership's debts and the partners' rights to share in the partnership's profits. Partnerships may use an assumed name, which must be filed with the register of deeds in the county in which the partnership does business.[37] Title to real property may be held in the partnership name, with a general partner executing the instrument on behalf of the partnership.[38] Each partner is individually liable for the acts and obligations of the partnership,[39] which is a major reason why partnerships are not as common for most business purposes as limited liability companies and corporations.

The ordinary partnership described above is sometimes referred to as a *general partnership*. Another form of partnership is the *limited partnership*, which consists of one or more general partners, who have rights and obligations, including liability, similar to partners in general partnerships, and one or more limited partners, whose authority is more limited and who are liable only to the extent of their investment in the limited partnership.[40] Unlike a general or ordinary partnership, a limited partnership cannot exist without a certificate of limited partnership executed and filed with the Department of the Secretary of State.[41] A limited partnership's name must include the words or abbreviation "limited partnership," "L.P.," "LP," or "ltd. partnership."[42] North Carolina limited partnerships must have a registered office and agent in the state.[43] A general partner of a limited partnership has the authority to bind the entity.[44]

A *registered limited liability partnership* is a form of partnership in which the general partners are not individually liable for the errors or omissions of other partners.[45] A registered limited liability partnership name must include the words "registered limited liability partnership" or "limited liability partnership" or the abbreviation "L.L.P.," "R.L.L.P.," "LLP," or "RLLP."[46] Similarly, to limit the liability of a general partner, a limited partnership can become a *limited liability limited partnership* by registering as such with the Department.[47] Its name must include the words "registered limited liability limited partnership," or "limited liability limited partnership" or the abbreviation "L.L.L.P.," R.L.L.L.P.," "LLLP," or "RLLLP."[48]

A *trust* is created with an agreement between someone transferring property or rights to property to another with the intent that the property be held for the transferor's benefit. The person who transfers the property or property right is the *settlor*, *grantor*, *trustor*, or *creator*. The person entrusted is the *trustee*. Trustees may be individuals, groups of individuals, or institutions, such as banks. The person or entity for whose benefit the property is entrusted is the *beneficiary*. Trusts are governed by *trust agreements*, which may be separate documents or contained within wills. Trustees, as fiduciaries, are subject to strict statutory and common law obligations.

---

37. G.S. 66-68(a).
38. G.S. 59-40.
39. G.S. 59-45(a).
40. G.S. 59-303.
41. G.S. 59-201(a).
42. G.S. 55D-20(a)(2).
43. G.S. 55D-30.
44. G.S. 59-403.
45. G.S. 59-45.
46. G.S. 55D-20(a)(5).
47. G.S. 59-210.
48. G.S. 55D-20(a)(4).

Religious organizations may appoint trustees to acquire, hold, and convey property in trust for a church, denomination, religious society, or congregation.[49] These organizations may also act through their ecclesiastical officers.[50]

These are common types of organizations or entities that a notary may encounter. There are other organizations authorized by state or federal law, each of which is governed by particular laws and requirements. If a notary has reason to question the legitimacy of any organization, he or she should consult with qualified legal counsel.

5.5 Motor Vehicle Titles

A North Carolina resident who intends to operate a motor vehicle on a state highway must register the vehicle with the Division of Motor Vehicles of the Department of Transportation.[51] Only an owner with a certificate of title may register a vehicle. Although one person may sell another a motor vehicle by private agreement, title is transferred only when the registration and certificate of title process is completed. This process requires an assignment of title from the seller to the buyer. An owner of a vehicle subject to registration must apply to the Division of Motor Vehicles for a certificate of title, a registration plate, and a registration card for the vehicle.[52] Assignments of and applications for a North Carolina title require acknowledgments.

Security interests in motor vehicles, which commonly are used as collateral for money loaned for the vehicle's purchase, may be perfected only with a notation on the certificate of title issued by the Division of Motor Vehicles.[53] Motor vehicles are the subjects of much theft and fraud, and the procedures for obtaining and transferring title are subject to strict requirements and formalities.

---

49. G.S. 61-2.
50. G.S. 61-5.
51. G.S. 20-50(a).
52. G.S. 20-52.
53. G.S. 20-58.

APPENDIX 1

TEXT OF GENERAL STATUTES

Effective October 1, 2006

(Note: This text reflects the statutes as revised by 2006 legislation. The final provisions of the General Statutes may contain variations from what is depicted here and in this guidebook's citations, including renumbering, due to technical corrections made in the final compilation.)

Chapter 10B.

Article 1

Notary Public Act

Notaries.

Part 1. General Provisions.

§ 10B-1. Short title.
This Article is the "Notary Public Act" and may be cited by that name.

§ 10B-2. Purposes.
This Chapter shall be construed and applied to advance its underlying purposes, which are the following:
    (1) To promote, serve, and protect the public interests.
    (2) To simplify, clarify, and modernize the law governing notaries.
    (3) To prevent fraud and forgery.
    (4) To foster ethical conduct among notaries.
    (5) To enhance interstate recognition of notarial acts.
    (6) To integrate procedures for traditional paper and electronic notarial acts.

§ 10B-3. Definitions.

The following definitions apply in this Chapter:

(1) Acknowledgment. – A notarial act in which a notary certifies that at a single time and place all of the following occurred:

    a.   An individual appeared in person before the notary and presented a record.

    b.   The individual was personally known to the notary or identified by the notary through satisfactory evidence.

    c.   The individual did either of the following:

        i.   Indicated to the notary that the signature on the record was the individual's signature.

        ii.   Signed the record while in the physical presence of the notary and while being personally observed signing the record by the notary.

(2) Affirmation. – A notarial act which is legally equivalent to an oath and in which a notary certifies that at a single time and place all of the following occurred:

    a.   An individual appeared in person before the notary.

    b.   The individual was personally known to the notary or identified by the notary through satisfactory evidence.

    c.   The individual made a vow of truthfulness on penalty of perjury, based on personal honor and without invoking a deity or using any form of the word "swear".

(3) Attest or attestation. – The completion of a certificate by a notary who has performed a notarial act.

(4) Commission. – The empowerment to perform notarial acts and the written evidence of authority to perform those acts.

(5) Credible witness. – An individual who is personally known to the notary and to whom all of the following also apply:

    a.   The notary believes the individual to be honest and reliable for the purpose of confirming to the notary the identity of another individual.

    b.   The notary believes the individual is not a party to or beneficiary of the transaction.

(6) Department. – The North Carolina Department of the Secretary of State.

(7) Director. – The Division Director for the North Carolina Department of the Secretary of State Notary Public Section.

(8) Jurat. – A notary's certificate evidencing the administration of an oath or affirmation.

(9) Moral turpitude. – Conduct contrary to expected standards of honesty, morality, or integrity.

(10) Nickname. – A descriptive, familiar, or shortened form of a proper name.

(11) Notarial act, notary act, and notarization. – The act of taking an acknowledgment, taking a verification or proof or administering an oath or affirmation that a notary is empowered to perform under G.S. 10B-20(a).

(12) Notarial certificate and certificate. – The portion of a notarized record that is completed by the notary, bears the notary's signature and seal, and states the facts attested by the notary in a particular notarization.

(13) Notary public and notary. – A person commissioned to perform notarial acts under this Chapter. A notary is a public officer of the State of North Carolina and shall act in full and strict compliance with this act.

(14) Oath. – A notarial act which is legally equivalent to an affirmation and in which a notary certifies that at a single time and place all of the following occurred:
   a.   An individual appeared in person before the notary.
   b.   The individual was personally known to the notary or identified by the notary through satisfactory evidence.
   c.   The individual made a vow of truthfulness on penalty of perjury while invoking a deity or using any form of the word "swear".
(15) Official misconduct. – Either of the following:
   a.   A notary's performance of a prohibited act or failure to perform a mandated act set forth in this Chapter or any other law in connection with notarization.
   b.   A notary's performance of a notarial act in a manner found by the Secretary to be negligent or against the public interest.
(16) Personal appearance and appear in person before a notary. – An individual and a notary are in close physical proximity to one another so that they may freely see and communicate with one another and exchange records back and forth during the notarization process.
(17) Personal knowledge or personally know. – Familiarity with an individual resulting from interactions with that individual over a period of time sufficient to eliminate every reasonable doubt that the individual has the identity claimed.
(18) Principal. – One of the following:
   a.   In the case of an acknowledgment, the individual whose identity and due execution of a record is being certified by the notary.
   b.   In the case of a verification or proof, the individual other than a subscribing witness, whose:
       i.   Identity and due execution of the record is being proven; or
       ii. Signature is being identified as genuine.
   c.   In the case of an oath or affirmation, the individual who makes a vow of truthfulness on penalty of perjury.
(19) Record. – Information that is inscribed on a tangible medium and called a traditional or paper record.
(20) Regular place of work or business. – A location, office or other workspace, where an individual regularly spends all or part of the individual's work time.
(21) Revocation. – The cancellation of the notary's commission stated in the order of revocation.
(22) Satisfactory evidence. – Identification of an individual based on either of the following:
   a.   At least one current document issued by a federal, state, or federal or state-recognized tribal government agency bearing the photographic image of the individual's face and either the signature or a physical description of the individual.
   b.   The oath or affirmation of one credible witness who personally knows the individual seeking to be identified.
(23) Seal or stamp. – A device for affixing on a paper record an image containing a notary's name, the words "notary public," and other information as required in G.S. 10B-37.
(24) Secretary. – The North Carolina Secretary of State or the Secretary's designee.

(25)

(26) Subscribing witness. – A person who signs a record for the purpose of being a witness to the principal's execution of the record or to the principal's acknowledgment of his or her execution of the record. A subscribing witness may give proof of the execution of the record as provided in subdivision (28) of this section.

(27) Suspension and restriction. – The termination of a notary's commission for a period of time stated in an order of restriction or suspension. The terms "restriction" or "suspension" or a combination of both terms shall be used synonymously.

(28) Verification or proof. – A notarial act in which a notary certifies that all of the following occurred:

    a.   An individual appeared in person before the notary.

    b.   The individual was personally known to the notary or identified by the notary through satisfactory evidence.

    c.   The individual was not a party to or beneficiary of the transaction.

    d.   The individual took an oath or gave an affirmation and testified to one of the following:

        i. The individual is a subscribing witness and the principal who signed the record did so while being personally observed by the subscribing witness.

        ii. The individual is a subscribing witness and the principal who signed the record acknowledged his or her signature to the subscribing witness.

        iii. The individual recognized either the signature on the record of the principal or the signature on the record of the subscribing witness and the signature was genuine.

Part 2. Commissioning.

§ 10B-5. Qualifications.

    (a) Except as provided in subsection (d) of this section, the Secretary shall commission as a notary any qualified person who submits an application in accordance with this Chapter.

    (b) A person qualified for a notarial commission shall meet all of the following requirements:

        (1) Be at least 18 years of age or legally emancipated as defined in Article 35 of Chapter 7B of the General Statutes.

        (2) Reside or have a regular place of work or business in this State.

        (3) Reside legally in the United States.

        (4) Speak, read, and write the English language.

        (5) Possess a high school diploma or equivalent.

        (6) Pass the course of instruction described in this Article, unless the person is a licensed member of the North Carolina State Bar.

        (7) Purchase and keep as a reference the most recent manual approved by the Secretary that describes the duties and authority of notaries public.

        (8) Submit an application containing no significant misstatement or omission of fact. The application form shall be provided by the Secretary

and be available at the register of deeds office in each county. Every application shall include the signature of the applicant written with pen and ink, and the signature shall be acknowledged by the applicant before a person authorized to administer oaths.

(9) Obtain the recommendation of one publicly elected official in North Carolina and submit the recommendation with the application. The requirement of this subdivision shall not apply to any applicant who seeks to receive the oath of office from the register of deeds of a county where more than 15,000 active notaries public are on record on January 1 of the year when the application is filed.

(c) The notary shall be commissioned in his or her county of residence, unless the notary is not a North Carolina resident, in which case he or she shall be commissioned in the county of his or her employment or business.

(d) The Secretary may deny an application for commission or recommission if any of the following apply to an applicant:

(1) Submission of an incomplete application or an application containing material misstatement or omission of fact.

(2) The applicant's conviction or plea of admission or nolo contendere to a felony or any crime involving dishonesty or moral turpitude. In no case may a commission be issued to an applicant within 10 years after release from prison, probation, or parole, whichever is later.

(3) A finding or admission of liability against the applicant in a civil lawsuit based on the applicant's deceit.

(4) The revocation, suspension, restriction, or denial of a notarial commission or professional license by this or any other state or nation. In no case may a commission be issued to an applicant within five years after the completion of all conditions of any disciplinary order.

(5) A finding that the applicant has engaged in official misconduct, whether or not disciplinary action resulted.

(6) An applicant knowingly using false or misleading advertising in which the applicant as a notary represents that the applicant has powers, duties, rights, or privileges that the applicant does not possess by law.

(7) A finding by a state bar or court that the applicant has engaged in the unauthorized practice of law.

§ 10B-6. Application for commission.

Every application for a notary commission shall be made on paper with original signatures, or in another form determined by the Secretary, and shall include all of the following:

(1) A statement of the applicant's personal qualifications as required by this Chapter.

(2) A certificate or signed statement by the instructor evidencing successful completion of the course of instruction as required by this Chapter.

(3) A notarized declaration of the applicant, as required by this Chapter.

(4) Any other information that the Secretary deems appropriate.

(5) The application fee required by this Chapter.

§ 10B-7. Statement of personal qualification.

(a)   The application for a notary commission shall include at least all of the following:

(1)   The applicant's full legal name and the name to be used for commissioning, excluding nicknames.

(2)   The applicant's date of birth.

(3)   The mailing address for the applicant's residence, the street address for the applicant's residence, and the telephone number for the applicant's residence.

(4)   The applicant's county of residence.

(5)   The name of the applicant's employer, the street and mailing address for the applicant's employer, and telephone number for the applicant's employer.

(6)   The applicant's last four digits of the applicant's social security number.

(7)   The applicant's personal and business e-mail addresses.

(8)   A declaration that the applicant is a citizen of the United States or proof of the applicant's legal residency in this country.

(9)   A declaration that the applicant can speak, read, and writes in the English language.

(10)   A complete listing of any issuances, denials, revocations, suspensions, restrictions, and resignations of a notarial commission, professional license, or public office involving the applicant in this or any other state or nation.

(11)   A complete listing of any criminal convictions of the applicant, including any pleas of admission or nolo contendere, in this or any other state or nation.

(12)   A complete listing of any civil findings or admissions of fault or liability regarding the applicant's activities as a notary, in this or any other state or nation.

(b)   The information provided in an application that relates to subdivisions (2), (3), (6), and (7) of subsection (a) of this section shall be considered confidential information and shall not be subject to disclosure under Chapter 132 of the General Statutes.

§ 10B-8. Course of study and examination.

(a)   Every applicant for an initial notary commission shall, within the three months preceding application, take a course of classroom instruction of not less than six hours approved by the Secretary and take a written examination approved by the Secretary. An applicant must answer at least eighty percent (80%) of the questions correctly in order to pass the exam. This subsection shall not apply to a licensed member of the North Carolina State Bar.

(b)   Every applicant for recommissioning shall pass a written examination approved by and administered by or under the direction of the Secretary, unless the person is a licensed member of the North Carolina State Bar.

(c)   The content of the course of instruction and the written examinations shall be notarial laws, procedures, and ethics.

(d)   The Secretary may charge such fees as are reasonably necessary to pay the cost associated with developing and administering examinations permitted by this Chapter and for conducting the training of notaries and notary instructors.

§ 10B-9. Length of term and jurisdiction.

A person commissioned under this Chapter may perform notarial acts in any part of this State for a term of five years, unless the commission is earlier revoked or resigned. No commissions shall be effective prior to the administration of the oath of office. Any notarial acts performed before the administration of the oath of office, either the original commissioning or recommissioning, are invalid.

§ 10B-10. Commission; oath of office.

(a) If the Secretary grants a commission to an applicant, the Secretary shall notify the appointee and shall instruct the appointee regarding the proper procedure for taking the oath at the register of deeds office in the county of the appointee's commissioning.

(b) The appointee shall appear before the register of deeds no later than 45 days after commissioning and shall be duly qualified by taking the general oath of office prescribed in G.S. 11-11 and the oath prescribed for officers in G.S. 11-7.

(c) After the appointee qualifies by taking the oath of office required under subsection (b) of this section, the register of deeds shall place the notary record in a book designated for that purpose, or the notary record may be recorded in the Consolidated Document Book and indexed in the Consolidated Real Property Index under the notary's name in the grantor index. The notary record may be kept in electronic format so long as the signature of the notary public may be viewed and printed. The notary record shall contain the name and the signature of the notary as commissioned, the effective date and expiration date of the commission, the date the oath was administered, and the date of any restriction, suspension, revocation, or resignation. The record shall constitute the official record of the qualification of notaries public.

(d) The register of deeds shall deliver the commission to the notary following completion of the requirements of this section and shall notify the Secretary of the delivery.

(e) If the appointee does not appear before the register of deeds within 45 days of commissioning, the register of deeds must return the commission to the Secretary, and the appointee must reapply for commissioning. If the appointee reapplies within one year of the granting of the commission, the Secretary may waive the educational requirements of this Chapter.

§ 10B-11. Recommissioning.

(a) A commissioned notary may apply for recommissioning no earlier than 10 weeks prior to the expiration date of the notary's commission.

(b) A notary whose commission has not expired must comply with the following requirements to be recommissioned:

(1) Submit a new application meeting the requirements of G.S. 10B-6, except for G.S. 10B-6(2).

(2) Meet all the requirements of G.S. 10B-5(b), except for G.S. 10B-5(b)(5), (6), and (9).

(3) Achieve a passing score on the written examination required under G.S. 10B-8(b). This requirement does not apply if the notary is a licensed member of the North Carolina State Bar, or if the notary has been continuously

commissioned in North Carolina since July 10, 1991, and has never been disciplined by the Secretary.

(c) An individual may apply for recommissioning within one year after the expiration of the individual's commission. The individual must comply with the requirement of subsection (b) of this section. The individual must also fulfill the educational requirement under G.S. 10B-8(a), unless the Secretary waives that requirement.

§ 10B-12. Notarized declaration.

The application for a notary public commission shall contain the following declaration to be executed by each applicant under oath:

Declaration of Applicant

I, _____ (name of applicant), solemnly swear or affirm under penalty of perjury that the information in this application is true, complete, and correct; that I understand the official duties and responsibilities of a notary public in this State, as described in the statutes; and that I will perform to the best of my ability all notarial acts in accordance with the law.

_____
(signature of applicant)

§ 10B-13. Application fee.

Every applicant for a notary commission shall pay to the Secretary a nonrefundable application fee of fifty dollars ($50.00).

§ 10B-14. Instructor's certification.

(a) The course of study required by G.S. 10B-5(b) shall be taught by an instructor certified under rules adopted by the Secretary. An instructor must meet the following requirements to be certified to teach a course of study for notaries public:
  (1) Complete and pass an instructor certification course of not less than six hours taught by the Director or other person approved by the Secretary.
  (2) Have at least one year of active experience as a notary public.
  (3) Maintain a current commission as a notary public.
  (4) Possess the current notary public guidebook.
  (5) Pay a nonrefundable fee of fifty dollars ($50.00).

(b) Certification to teach a course of study for notaries shall be effective for two years. A certification may be renewed by passing a recertification course taught by the Director or other person approved by the Secretary and by paying a nonrefundable fee of fifty dollars ($50.00).

(c) The following individuals may be certified to teach a course of study for notaries public without paying the fee required by this section, and they may renew their certification without paying the renewal fee, so long as they remain actively employed in the capacities named:
  (1) Registers of deeds.
  (2) Clerks of court.
  (3) The Director and other duly authorized employees of the Secretary.

(d) Former registers of deeds and clerks of court who have been certified as notary public instructors must apply for commissioning as a notary public but are exempt from the education requirements of G.S. 10B-8 after successful completion of an examination administered by the Secretary.

(e) Assistant and deputy registers of deeds and assistant and deputy clerks of court must have a regular notary commission prior to receiving a certification or recertification as a notary public instructor.

(f) The Secretary may suspend or revoke the certification of a notary instructor for violating the provisions of this Chapter or any of the administrative rules implementing it.

Part 3. Notarial Acts, Powers, and Limitations.

§ 10B-20. Powers and limitations.

(a) A notary may perform any of the following notarial acts:
    (1) Acknowledgments.
    (2) Oaths and affirmations.
    (3) Verifications or proofs.

(b) A notarial act shall be attested by all of the following:
    (1) The signature of the notary, exactly as shown on the notary's commission.
    (2) The legible appearance of the notary's name exactly as shown on the notary's commission. The legible appearance of the name may be ascertained from the notary's typed or printed name near the notary's signature or from elsewhere in the notarial certificate or from the notary's seal if the name is legible.
    (3) The clear and legible appearance of the notary's stamp or seal.
    (4) A statement of the date the notary's commission expires. The statement of the date that the notary's commission expires may appear in the notary's stamp or seal or elsewhere in the notarial certificate.

(c) A notary shall not perform a notarial act if any of the following apply:
    (1) The principal or subscribing witness is not in the notary's presence at the time the notarial act is performed. However, nothing in this Chapter shall require a notary to complete the notarial certificate attesting to the notarial act in the presence of the principal or subscribing witness.
    (2) The principal or subscribing witness is not personally known to the notary or identified by the notary through satisfactory evidence.
    (2a) The credible witness is not personally known to the notary.
    (5) The notary is a signer of, party to, or beneficiary of the record, that is to be notarized. However, a disqualification under this subdivision shall not apply to a notary who is named in a record solely as the trustee in a deed of trust, the drafter of the record, the person to whom a registered document should be mailed or sent after recording, or the attorney for a party to the record, so long as the notary is not also a party to the record individually or in some other representative or fiduciary capacity.
    (6) The notary will receive directly from a transaction connected with the notarial act any commission, fee, advantage, right, title, interest, cash, property, or other consideration exceeding in value the fees specified in

G.S. 10B-31, other than fees or other consideration paid for services rendered by a licensed attorney, a licensed real estate broker or salesperson, a motor vehicle dealer, or a banker.

(d) A notary may certify the affixation of a signature by mark on a record presented for notarization if:

(1) The mark is affixed in the presence of the notary;

(2) The notary writes below the mark: "Mark affixed by (name of signer by mark) in presence of undersigned notary"; and

(3) The notary notarizes the signature by performing an acknowledgment, oath or affirmation, jurat, or verification or proof.

(e) If a principal is physically unable to sign or make a mark on a record presented for notarization, that principal may designate another person as his or her designee, who shall be a disinterested party, to sign on the principal's behalf pursuant to the following procedure:

(1) The principal directs the designee to sign the record in the presence of the notary and two witnesses unaffected by the record;

(2) The designee signs the principal's name in the presence of the principal, the notary, and the two witnesses;

(3) Both witnesses sign their own names to the record near the principal's signature;

(4) The notary writes below the principal's signature: "Signature affixed by designee in the presence of (names and addresses of principal and witnesses)"; and

(5) The notary notarizes the signature through an acknowledgment, oath or affirmation, jurat, or verification or proof.

(f) A notarial act performed in another jurisdiction in compliance with the laws of that jurisdiction is valid to the same extent as if it had been performed by a notary commissioned under this Chapter if the notarial act is performed by a notary public of that jurisdiction or by any person authorized to perform notarial acts in that jurisdiction under the laws of that jurisdiction, the laws of this State, or federal law.

(g) Persons authorized by federal law or regulation to perform notarial acts may perform the acts for persons serving in or with the United States armed forces, their spouses, and their dependents.

(h) The Secretary and register of deeds in the county in which a notary qualified may certify to the commission of the notary.

(i) A notary public who is not an attorney licensed to practice law in this State who advertises the person's services as a notary public in a language other than English, by radio, television, signs, pamphlets, newspapers, other written communication, or in any other manner, shall post or otherwise include with the advertisement the notice set forth in this subsection in English and in the language used for the advertisement. The notice shall be of conspicuous size, if in writing, and shall state: "I AM NOT AN ATTORNEY LICENSED TO PRACTICE LAW IN THE STATE OF NORTH CAROLINA, AND I MAY NOT GIVE LEGAL ADVICE OR ACCEPT FEES FOR LEGAL ADVICE." If the advertisement is by radio or television, the statement may be modified but must include substantially the same message.

(j)   A notary public who is not an attorney licensed to practice law in this State is prohibited from representing or advertising that the notary public is an "immigration consultant" or expert on immigration matters unless the notary public is an accredited representative of an organization recognized by the Board of Immigration Appeals pursuant to Title 8, Part 292, section 2(a-e) of the Code of Federal Regulations (8 C.F.R. § 292.2(a-e)).

(k)   A notary public who is not an attorney licensed to practice law in this State is prohibited from rendering any service that constitutes the unauthorized practice of law. A nonattorney notary shall not assist another person in drafting, completing, selecting, or understanding a record or transaction requiring a notarial act.

(l)   A notary public required to comply with the provisions of subsection (i) of this section shall prominently post at the notary public's place of business a schedule of fees established by law, which a notary public may charge. The fee schedule shall be written in English and in the non-English language in which the notary services were solicited and shall contain the notice required in subsection (i) of this section, unless the notice is otherwise prominently posted at the notary public's place of business.

(m)   If notarial certificate wording is not provided or indicated for a record, a notary who is not also a licensed attorney shall not determine the type of notarial act or certificate to be used. This does not prohibit a notary from offering the selection of certificate forms recognized in this Chapter or as otherwise authorized by law.

(n)   A notary shall not claim to have powers, qualifications, rights, or privileges that the office of notary does not provide, including the power to counsel on immigration matters.

(o)   Before signing a notarial certificate and except as provided in this subsection, a notary shall cross out or mark through all blank lines or spaces in the certificate. However:

   (1)   Notwithstanding the provisions of this section, a notary shall not be required to complete, cross out, or mark through blank lines or spaces in the notary certificate form provided for in G.S. 47-43 indicating when and where a power of attorney is recorded if that recording information is not known to the notary at the time the notary completes and signs the certificate;

   (2)   A notary's failure to cross out or mark through blank lines or spaces in a notarial certificate shall not affect the sufficiency, validity, or enforceability of the certificate or the related record; and

   (3)   A notary's failure to cross out or mark through blank lines or spaces in a notarial certificate shall not be grounds for a register of deeds to refuse to accept a record for registration.

§ 10B-21. Notaries ex officio.

(a) The clerks of the superior court may act as notaries public in their several counties by virtue of their offices as clerks and may certify their notarial acts only under the seals of their respective courts. Assistant and deputy clerks of superior court, by virtue of their offices, may perform the following notarial acts and may certify these notarial acts only under the seals of their respective courts:

    (1) Oaths and affirmations.

    (2) Verifications or proofs.

    Upon completion of the course of study provided for in G.S. 10B-5(b), assistant and deputy clerks of superior court may, by virtue of their offices, perform all other notarial acts and may certify these notarial acts only under the seals of their respective courts. A course of study attended only by assistant and deputy clerks of superior court may be taught at any mutually convenient location agreed to by the Secretary and the Administrative Office of the Courts.

(b) Registers of deeds may act as notaries public in their several counties by virtue of their offices as registers of deeds and may certify their notarial acts only under the seals of their respective offices. Assistant and deputy registers of deeds, by virtue of their offices, may perform the following notarial acts and may certify these notarial acts only under the seals of their respective offices:

    (1) Oaths and affirmations.

    (2) Verifications or proofs.

    Upon completion of the course of study provided for in G.S. 10B-5(b), assistant and deputy registers of deeds may, by virtue of their offices, perform all other notarial acts and may certify these notarial acts only under the seals of their respective offices. A course of study attended only by assistant and deputy registers of deeds may be taught at any mutually convenient location agreed to by the Secretary and the North Carolina Association of Registers of Deeds.

(c) The Director may act as a notary public by virtue of the Director's employment in the Department of the Secretary and may certify a notarial act performed in that capacity under the seal of the Secretary.

(d) Unless otherwise provided by law, a person designated a notary public by this section may charge a fee for a notarial act performed in accordance with G.S. 10B-31. The fee authorized by this section is payable to the governmental unit or agency by whom the person is employed.

(e) Nothing in this section shall authorize a person to act as a notary public other than in the performance of the official duties of the person's office unless the person complies fully with the requirements of G.S. 10B-5.

§ 10B-22. False certificate; foreign language certificates.

(a) A notary shall not execute a notarial certificate containing information known or believed by the notary to be false.

(b) A notary shall not execute a certificate that is not written in the English language. A notary may execute a certificate written in the English language that accompanies a record written in another language, which record may include a translation of the notarial certificate into the other language. In those instances, the notary shall execute only the English language certificate.

§ 10B-23. Improper records.

(a) A notary shall not notarize a signature on a record without a notarial certificate indicating what type of notarial act was performed. However, a notary may administer an oath or affirmation without completing a jurat.

(b) A notary shall neither certify, notarize, nor authenticate a photograph. A notary may notarize an affidavit regarding and attached to a photograph.

§ 10B-24. Testimonials.

A notary shall not use the official notary title or seal in a manner intended to endorse, promote, denounce, or oppose any product, service, contest, candidate, or other offering. This section does not prohibit a notary public from performing a notarial act upon a record executed by another individual.

Part 4. Fees.

§ 10B-30. Imposition and waiver of fees.

(a) For performing a notarial act, a notary may charge up to the maximum fee specified in this Chapter.

(b) A notary shall not discriminatorily condition the fee for a notarial act on any attribute of the principal that would constitute unlawful discrimination.

(c) Nothing in this Chapter shall compel a notary to charge a fee.

§ 10B-31. Fees for notarial acts.

The maximum fees that may be charged by a notary for notarial acts are as follows:

(1) For acknowledgments, jurats, verifications or proofs, five dollars ($5.00) per principal signature.

(2) For oaths or affirmations without a signature, five dollars ($5.00) per person, except for an oath or affirmation administered to a credible witness to vouch for the identity of a principal or subscribing witness.

§ 10B-32. Notice of fees.

Notaries who charge for their notarial services shall conspicuously display in their places of business, or present to each principal outside their places of business, an English-language schedule of fees for notarial acts. No part of any notarial fee schedule shall be printed in smaller than 10-point type.

Part 5. Signature and Seal.

§ 10B-35. Official signature.

When notarizing a paper record, a notary shall sign by hand in ink on the notarial certificate. The notary shall comply with the requirements of G.S. 10B-20(b)(1) and (b)(2). The notary shall affix the official signature only after the notarial act is performed. The notary shall not sign a paper record using the facsimile stamp or an electronic or other printing method.

§ 10B-36. Official seal.

(a) A notary shall keep an official seal or stamp that is the exclusive property of the notary. The notary shall keep the seal in a secure location. A notary shall not allow another person to use or possess the seal, and shall not surrender the seal to the notary's employer upon termination of employment.

(b) The seal shall be affixed only after the notarial act is performed. The notary shall place the image or impression of the seal near the notary's signature on every paper record notarized. The seal and the notary's signature shall appear on the same page of a record as the text of the notarial certificate.

(c) A notary shall do the following within 10 days of discovering that the notary's seal has been lost or stolen:

    (1) Inform the appropriate law enforcement agency in the case of theft or vandalism.

    (2) Notify the appropriate register of deeds and the Secretary in writing and signed in the official name in which he or she was commissioned.

(d) As soon as is reasonably practicable after resignation, revocation, or expiration of a notary commission, or death of the notary, the seal shall be delivered to the Secretary for disposal.

§ 10B-37. Seal image.

(a) A notary shall affix the notary's official seal near the notary's official signature on the notarial certificate of a record.

(b) A notary's official seal shall include all of the following elements:

    (1) The notary's name exactly as commissioned.

    (2) The words "Notary Public".

    (3) The county of commissioning, including the word "County" or the abbreviation "Co.".

    (4) The words "North Carolina" or the abbreviation "NC".

(c) The notary seal may be either circular or rectangular in shape. Upon receiving a commission or a recommission on or after October 1, 2006, a notary shall not use a circular seal that is less than 1 1/2 inches, nor more than 2 inches in diameter. The rectangular seal shall not be over 1 inch high and 2 1/2 inches long. The perimeter of the seal shall contain a border that is visible when impressed.

(c1) Alterations to any information contained within the seal as embossed or stamped on the record are prohibited.

(d) A notarial seal, as it appears on a record, may contain the permanently imprinted, handwritten, or typed date the notary's commission expires.

(e) Any reference in the General Statutes to the seal of a notary shall include the stamp of a notary, and any reference to the stamp of a notary shall include the seal of the notary.

(f) The failure of a notarial seal to comply with the requirements of this section shall not affect the sufficiency, validity, or enforceability of the notarial certificate, but shall constitute a violation of the notary's duties.

Part 6. Certificate Forms.

§ 10B-40. Notarial certificates in general.

(a) A notary shall not make or give a notarial certificate unless the notary has either personal knowledge or satisfactory evidence of the identity of the principal or, if applicable, the subscribing witness.

(a1) By making or giving a notarial certificate, whether or not stated in the certificate, a notary certifies as follows:

(1) As to an acknowledgment, all those things described in G.S. 10B-3(1).

(2) As to an affirmation, all those things described in G.S. 10B-3(2).

(3) As to an oath, all those things described in G.S. 10B-3(14).

(4) As to a verification or proof, all those things described in G.S. 10B-3(28).

(a2) In addition to the certifications under subsection (a1) of this section, by making or giving a notarial certificate, whether or not stated in the certificate, a notary certifies to all of the following:

(1) At the time the notarial act was performed and the notarial certificate was signed by the notary, the notary was lawfully commissioned, the notary's commission had neither expired nor been suspended, the notarial act was performed within the geographic limits of the notary's commission, and the notarial act was performed in accordance with the provision of this Chapter.

(2) If the notarial certificate is for an acknowledgment or the administration of an oath or affirmation, the person whose signature was notarized did not appear in the judgment of the notary to be incompetent, lacking in understanding of the nature and consequences of the transaction requiring the notarial act, or acting involuntarily, under duress, or undue influence.

(3) The notary was not prohibited from acting under G.S. 10-20(c).

(a3) The inclusion of additional information in a notarial certificate, including the representative or fiduciary capacity in which a person signed or the means a notary used to identify a principal, shall not invalidate an otherwise sufficient notarial certificate.

(b) A notarial certificate for the acknowledgment taken by a notary of a principal who is an individual acting in his or her own right or who is an individual acting in a representative or fiduciary capacity is sufficient and shall be accepted in this State if it is substantially in the form set forth in G.S. 10B-41, if it is substantially in a form otherwise prescribed by the laws of this State, or if it includes all of the following:

(1) Identifies the state and county in which the acknowledgment occurred.

(2) Names the principal who appeared in person before the notary.

(4) Indicates that the principal appeared in person before the notary and the principal acknowledged that he or she signed the record.

(5) States the date of the acknowledgment.

(6) Contains the signature and seal or stamp of the notary who took the acknowledgment.

(7) States the notary's commission expiration date.

(c) A notarial certificate for the verification or proof of the signature of a principal by a subscribing witness taken by a notary is sufficient and shall be accepted in this State if it is substantially in the form set forth in G.S. 10B-42, if it is substantially in a form otherwise prescribed by the laws of this State, or if it includes all of the following:

(1) Identifies the state and county in which the verification or proof occurred.

(2) Names the subscribing witness who appeared in person before the notary.

(4) Names the principal whose signature on the record is to be verified or proven.

(5) Indicates that the subscribing witness certified to the notary under oath or by affirmation that the subscribing witness is not a party to or beneficiary of the transaction, signed the record as a subscribing witness, and either (i) witnessed the principal sign the record, or (ii) witnessed the principal acknowledge the principal's signature on the record.

(6) States the date of the verification or proof.

(7) Contains the signature and seal or stamp of the notary who took the verification or proof.

(8) States the notary's commission expiration date.

(c1) A notarial certificate for the verification or proof of the signature of a principal or a subscribing witness by a nonsubscribing witness taken by a notary is sufficient and shall be accepted in this State if it is substantially in the form set forth in G.S. 10B-42.1, if it is substantially in a form otherwise prescribed by the laws of this State, or if it includes all of the following:

(1) Identifies the state and county in which the verification or proof occurred.

(2) Names the nonsubscribing witness who appeared in person before the notary.

(3) Names the principal or subscribing witness whose signature on the record is to be verified or proven.

(4) Indicates that the nonsubscribing witness certified to the notary under oath or by affirmation that the nonsubscribing witness is not a party to or beneficiary of the transaction and that the nonsubscribing witness recognizes the signature of either the principal or the subscribing witness and that the signature is genuine.

(5) States the date of the verification or proof.

(6) Contains the signature and seal or stamp of the notary who took the verification or proof.

(7) States the notary's commission expiration date.

(d) A notarial certificate for an oath or affirmation taken by a notary is sufficient and shall be accepted in this State if it is substantially in the form set forth in G.S. 10B-43, if it is substantially in a form otherwise prescribed by the laws of this State, or if it includes all of the following:

(2) Names the principal who appeared in person before the notary unless the name of the principal otherwise is clear from the record itself.

(4) Indicates that the principal who appeared in person before the notary signed the record in question and certified to the notary under oath or by affirmation as to the truth of the matters stated in the record.

(5) States the date of the oath or affirmation.

    (6)   Contains the signature and seal or stamp of the notary who took the oath or affirmation.

    (7)   States the notary's commission expiration date.

(e) Any notarial certificate made in another jurisdiction shall be sufficient in this State if it is made in accordance with federal law or the laws of the jurisdiction where the notarial certificate is made.

(f) On records to be filed, registered, recorded, or delivered in another state or jurisdiction of the United States, a North Carolina notary may complete any notarial certificate that may be required in that other state or jurisdiction.

(g) Nothing in this Chapter shall be deemed to authorize the use of a notarial certificate authorized by this Part in place of or as an alternative to a notarial certificate required by any other provision of the General Statutes outside of Chapter 47 of the General Statutes that prescribes the specific form or content for a notarial certificate including G.S. 31-11.6, Chapter 32A of the General Statutes, and G.S. 90-321. However, any statute that permits or requires the use of a notarial certificate contained within Chapter 47 of the General Statutes may also be satisfied by the use of a notarial certificate permitted by this Part. Any form of acknowledgment or probate authorized under Chapter 47 of the General Statutes shall be conclusively deemed in compliance with the requirements of this section.

(h) If an individual signs a record and purports to be acting in a representative or fiduciary capacity, that individual is also deemed to represent to the notary that he or she is signing the record with proper authority to do so and also is signing the record on behalf of the person or entity represented and identified therein or in the fiduciary capacity indicated therein. In performing a notarial act in relation to an individual described under this subsection, a notary is under no duty to verify whether the individual acted in a representative or fiduciary capacity or, if so, whether the individual was duly authorized so to do. A notarial certificate may include any of the following:

    (1)   A statement that an individual signed a record in a particular representative or fiduciary capacity.

    (2)   A statement that the individual who signed the record in a representative or fiduciary capacity had due authority so to do.

    (3)   A statement identifying the represented person or entity or the fiduciary capacity.

§ 10B-41. Notarial certificate for an acknowledgment.

(a) When properly completed by a notary, a notarial certificate that substantially complies with the following form may be used and shall be sufficient under the law of this State to satisfy the requirements for a notarial certificate for the acknowledgment of a principal who is an individual acting in his or her own right or who is an individual acting in a representative or fiduciary capacity. The authorization of the form in this section does not preclude the use of other forms.

_____ County, North Carolina

I certify that the following person(s) personally appeared before me this day, each acknowledging to me that he or she signed the foregoing document: *name(s) of principal(s)*.

Date: _____   *Official Signature of Notary*
                                                  Notary's printed or typed name, Notary Public
(Official Seal)   My commission expires: _____

(c) The notary's printed or typed name as shown in the form provided in sub-section (a) of this section is not required if the legible appearance of the notary's name may be ascertained from the notary's typed or printed name near the notary's signature or from elsewhere in the notarial certificate or from the notary's seal if the name is legible.

§ 10B-42. Notarial certificate for a verification of subscribing witness.

(a) When properly completed by a notary, a notarial certificate in substantially the following form may be used and shall be sufficient under the law of this State to satisfy the requirements for a notarial certificate for the verification or proof of the signature of a principal by a subscribing witness. The authoriza-tion of the form in this section does not preclude the use of other forms.

_____ County, North Carolina

I certify that *(name of subscribing witness)* personally appeared before me this day and certified to me under oath or by affirmation that he or she is not a grantee or beneficiary of the transaction, signed the foregoing document as a subscribing witness, and either (i) witnessed *(name of principal)* sign the fore-going document or (ii) witnessed *(name of principal)* acknowledge his or her signature on the already-signed document.

Date: _____   *Official Signature of Notary*
                                                  Notary's printed or typed name, Notary Public
(Official Seal)   My commission expires: _____

(c) The notary's printed or typed name as shown in the form provided in sub-section (a) of this section is not required if the legible appearance of the notary's name may be ascertained from the notary's typed or printed name near the notary's signature or from elsewhere in the notarial certificate or from the notary's seal if the name is legible.

§ 10B-42.1 Notarial certificate for a verification of nonsubscribing witness.

(a) When properly completed by a notary, a notarial certificate in substantially the following form may be used and shall be sufficient under the law of this State to satisfy the requirements for a notarial certificate for the verification or proof of the signature of a principal or subscribing witness by a nonsubscribing witness. The authorization of the form in this section does not preclude the use of other forms.

_____ County, North Carolina

I certify that (*name of nonsubscribing witness*) personally appeared before me this day and certified to me under oath or by affirmation that he or she is not a grantee or beneficiary of the transaction, that (*name of nonsubscribing witness*) recognizes the signature of (*name of the principal or the subscribing witness*) and that the signature is genuine.

Date: _____   *Official Signature of Notary*
                           Notary's printed or typed name, Notary Public
(Official Seal)   My commission expires: _____

(c) The notary's printed or typed name as shown in the form provided in subsection (a) of this section is not required if the legible appearance of the notary's name may be ascertained from the notary's typed or printed name near the notary's signature or from elsewhere in the notarial certificate or from the notary's seal if the name is legible.

§ 10B-43. Notarial certificate for an oath or affirmation.
(a) When properly completed by a notary, a notarial certificate that substantially complies with either of the following forms may be used and shall be sufficient under the law of this State to satisfy the requirements for a notarial certificate for an oath or affirmation. The authorization of the forms in this section does not preclude the use of other forms.

_____ County, North Carolina

Signed and sworn to before me this day by *(name of principal)*.

Date: _____   *Official Signature of Notary*
                           Notary's printed or typed name, Notary Public
(*Official Seal*)   My commission expires: _____

—OR—

_____ County, North Carolina

Sworn to or subscribed before me this day by *(name of principal)*.

Date: _____   *Official Signature of Notary*
                           Notary's printed or typed name, Notary Public
(*Official Seal*)   My commission expires: _____

(c)   The notary's printed or typed name as shown in the form provided in sub-section (a) of this section is not required if the legible appearance of the notary's name may be ascertained from the notary's typed or printed name near the notary's signature or from elsewhere in the notarial certificate or from the notary's seal if the name is legible.

(d)   In either of the forms provided under subsection (a) of this section all of the following shall apply:

    (1)   The name of the principal may be omitted if the name of the principal is located near the jurat, and the principal who so appeared before the notary is clear from the record itself.

    (2)   The words "affirmed" or "sworn to or affirmed" may be substituted for the words "sworn to".

Part 7. Changes in Status.

§ 10B-50. Change of address.

Within 45 days after the change of a notary's residence, business, or any mailing address or telephone number, the notary shall send to the Secretary by fax, e-mail, or certified mail, return receipt requested, a signed notice of the change, giving both old and new addresses or telephone numbers.

§ 10B-51. Change of name.

(a)   Within 45 days after the legal change of a notary's name, the notary shall send to the Secretary by fax, e-mail, or certified mail, return receipt requested, a signed notice of the change. The notice shall include both the notary's former name and the notary's new name.

(b)   A notary with a new name may continue to use the former name in perform-ing notarial acts until all of the following steps have been completed:

    (1)   The notary receives a confirmation of Notary's Name Change from the Secretary.

    (2)   The notary obtains a new seal bearing the new name exactly as that name appears in the confirmation from the Secretary.

    (3)   The notary appears before the register of deeds to which the commission was delivered within 45 days of the effective date of the change to be duly qualified by taking the general oath of office prescribed in G.S. 11-11 and the oath prescribed for officers in G.S. 11-7 under the new name and to have the notary public record changed to reflect the new commissioned name.

(c)   Upon completion of the requirements in subsection (b) of this section, the notary shall use the new name.

§ 10B-52. Change of county.

(a)   A notary who has moved to another county in North Carolina remains com-missioned until the current commission expires, is not required to obtain a new seal, and may continue to notarize without changing his or her seal.

(b)   When a notary who has moved applies to be recommissioned, if the com-mission is granted, the Secretary shall issue a notice of recommissioning. The commission applicant shall then do all of the following:

    (1)   Obtain a new seal bearing the new county exactly as in the notice of recommissioning.

(2)   Appear before the register of deeds to which the commission was delivered within 45 days of recommissioning, to be duly qualified by taking the general oath of office prescribed in G.S. 11-11 and the oath prescribed for officers in G.S. 11-7 under the new county and to have the notary public record changed to reflect the new county name.

§ 10B-53. Change of both name and county.

Within 45 days after the legal change of a notary's name, and if the notary has also moved to a different county than as last commissioned, the notary shall submit to the Secretary a recommissioning application and fee pursuant to this Chapter. The notary may continue to perform notarial acts under the notary's previous name and seal until all of the following steps have been completed:

(1)   The notary receives a transmittal receipt of reappointment due to name and county change from the Secretary.

(2)   The notary obtains a new seal bearing the new name and county exactly as those items appear in the transmittal receipt.

(3)   The notary appears before the register of deeds to which the commission was delivered within 45 days of recommissioning to be duly qualified by taking the general oath of office prescribed in G.S. 11-11 and the oath prescribed for officers in G.S. 11-7 under the new name and county and to have the notary public record changed to reflect the new name and county.

§ 10B-54. Resignation.

(a)   A notary who resigns the notary's commission shall send to the Secretary by fax, e-mail, or certified mail, return receipt requested, a signed notice indicating the effective date of resignation.

(b)   Notaries who cease to reside in or to maintain a regular place of work or business in this State, or who become permanently unable to perform their notarial duties, shall resign their commissions and shall deliver their seals to the Secretary by certified mail, return receipt requested.

§ 10B-55. Disposition of seal; death of notary.

(a)   When a notary commission is resigned or revoked, the notary shall deliver the notary's seal to the Secretary within 45 days of the resignation or revocation. Delivery shall be accomplished by certified mail, return receipt requested. The Secretary shall destroy any seal received under this subsection.

(b)   A notary whose commission has expired and whose previous commission or application was not revoked or denied by this State, is not required to deliver the seal to the Secretary as provided under subsection (a) of this section if the notary intends to apply to be recommissioned and is recommissioned within three months after the notary's commission expires.

(c)   If a notary dies while commissioned or before fulfilling the disposition of seal requirements in this section, the notary's estate shall, as soon as is reasonably practicable and no later than the closing of the estate, notify the Secretary in writing of the notary's death and deliver the notary's seal to the Secretary for destruction.

Part 8. Enforcement, Sanctions, and Remedies.

§ 10B-60. Enforcement and penalties.

(a) The Secretary may issue a warning to a notary or restrict, suspend, or revoke a notarial commission for a violation of this Chapter and on any ground for which an application for a commission may be denied under this Chapter. Any period of restriction, suspension, or revocation shall not extend the expiration date of a commission.

(b) Except as otherwise permitted by law, a person who commits any of the following acts is guilty of a Class 1 misdemeanor:

   (1) Holding one's self out to the public as a notary if the person does not have a commission.

   (2) Performing a notarial act if the person's commission has expired or been suspended or restricted.

   (3) Performing a notarial act before the person had taken the oath of office.

(c) A notary shall be guilty of a Class 1 misdemeanor if the notary does any of the following:

   (1) Takes an acknowledgment or administers an oath or affirmation without the principal appearing in person before the notary.

   (2) Takes a verification or proof without the subscribing witness appearing in person before the notary.

   (3) Takes an acknowledgment or administers an oath or affirmation without personal knowledge or satisfactory evidence of the identity of the principal.

   (4) Takes a verification or proof without personal knowledge or satisfactory evidence of the identity of the subscribing witness.

(d) A notary shall be guilty of a Class I felony if the notary does any of the following:

   (1) Takes an acknowledgment or a verification or a proof, or administers an oath or affirmation if the notary knows it is false or fraudulent.

   (2) Takes an acknowledgment or administers an oath or affirmation without the principal appearing in person before the notary if the notary does so with the intent to commit fraud.

   (3) Takes a verification or proof without the subscribing witness appearing in person before the notary if the notary does so with the intent to commit fraud.

(e) It is a Class I felony for any person to perform notarial acts in this State with the knowledge that the person is not commissioned under this Chapter.

(f) Any person who without authority obtains, uses, conceals, defaces, or destroys the seal or notarial records of a notary is guilty of a Class I felony.

(g) For purposes of enforcing this Chapter and Article 34 of Chapter 66 of the General Statutes, the law enforcement agents of the Department of the Secretary of State have statewide jurisdiction and have all of the powers and authority of law enforcement officers. The agents have the authority to assist local law enforcement agencies in their investigations and to initiate and carry out, on their own or in coordination with local law enforcement agencies, investigations of violations.

(h) Resignation or expiration of a notarial commission does not terminate or preclude an investigation into a notary's conduct by the Secretary, who may pursue the investigation to a conclusion, whereupon it may be a matter of public record whether or not the finding would have been grounds for disciplinary action.

(i) The Secretary may seek injunctive relief against any person who violates the provisions of this Chapter. Nothing in this Chapter diminishes the authority of the North Carolina State Bar.

(j) Any person who knowingly solicits, coerces, or in any material way influences a notary to commit official misconduct, is guilty as an aider and abettor and is subject to the same level of punishment as the notary.

(k) The sanctions and remedies of this Chapter supplement other sanctions and remedies provided by law, including, but not limited to, forgery and aiding and abetting.

Part 9. Validation of Notarial Acts.

§ 10B-65. Acts of notaries public in certain instances validated.

(a) Any acknowledgment taken and any instrument notarized by a person prior to qualification as a notary public but after commissioning or recommissioning as a notary public, or by a person whose notary commission has expired, is hereby validated. The acknowledgment and instrument shall have the same legal effect as if the person qualified as a notary public at the time the person performed the act.

(b) All documents bearing a notarial seal and which contain any of the following errors are validated and given the same legal effect as if the errors had not occurred:

(1) The date of the expiration of the notary's commission is stated, whether correctly or erroneously.

(2) The notarial seal does not contain a readable impression of the notary's name, contains an incorrect spelling of the notary's name, or does not bear the name of the notary exactly as it appears on the commission, as required under G.S. 10B-37.

(3) The notary's signature does not comport exactly with the name on the notary commission or on the notary seal, as required by G.S. 10B-20.

(4) The notarial seal contains typed, printed, drawn, or handwritten material added to the seal, fails to contain the words "North Carolina" or the abbreviation "NC", or contains correct information except that instead of the abbreviation for North Carolina contains the abbreviation for another state.

(c) All deeds of trust in which the notary was named in the document as a trustee only are validated.

(d) All notary acknowledgments performed before January 1, 1953, bearing a notarial seal are hereby validated.

(e) This section applies to notarial acts performed on or before February 1, 2004.

§ 10B-66. Certain notarial acts validated.

(a) Any acknowledgment taken and any instrument notarized by a person whose notarial commission was revoked on or before January 30, 1997, is hereby validated.

(b) This section applies to notarial acts performed on or before August 1, 1998.

§ 10B-67. Erroneous commission expiration date cured.
An erroneous statement of the date that the notary's commission expires shall not affect the sufficiency, validity, or enforceability of the notarial certificate or the related record if the notary is, in fact, lawfully commissioned at the time of the notarial act.

§ 10B-68. Technical defects cured.
(a) Technical defects, errors, or omissions in a notarial certificate shall not affect the sufficiency, validity, or enforceability of the notarial certificate or the related instrument or document. This subsection applies to notarial certificates made on or after December 1, 2005.

(b) Defects in the commissioning or recommissioning of a notary that are approved by the Department are cured. This subsection applies to commissions and recommissions issued on or after December 1, 2005.

(c) As used in this section, a technical defect includes those cured under G.S. 10B-37(f) and G.S. 10B-67. Other technical defects include the absence of the legible appearance of the notary's name exactly as shown on the notary's commission as required in G.S. 10B-20(b). This subsection applies to notarial certificates made on or after December 1, 2005.

§ 10B-69. Official forms cured.
(a) The notarial certificate contained in a form issued by a State agency prior to October 1, 2006, is deemed to be a valid certificate provided the certificate complied with the law at the time the form was issued.

(b) The notarization using a certificate under subsection (a) of this section shall be deemed valid if executed in compliance with the law at the time the form was issued.

§ 10B-99. Presumption of regularity.
(a) In the absence of evidence of fraud on the part of the notary, or evidence of a knowing and deliberate violation of this Article by the notary, the courts shall grant a presumption of regularity to notarial acts so that those acts may be upheld, provided there has been substantial compliance with the law. Nothing in this Chapter modifies or repeals the common law doctrine of substantial compliance in effect on November 30, 2005.

(b) A notarial act performed before October 1, 2006, shall be deemed valid if it complies with the law as it existed on or before December 1, 2005.

Article 2

Electronic Notary Act

Part 1. General Provisions.

§ 10B-100. Short title.
This Article is the Electronic Notary Public Act and may be cited by that name.

§ 10B-101. Definitions.

The following definitions apply in this Article:

(1)   "Electronic" means relating to technology having electrical, digital, magnetic, wireless, optical, electromagnetic, or similar capabilities.

(2)   "Electronic Document" means information that is created, generated, sent, communicated, received, or stored by electronic means.

(3)   "Electronic Notarial Act" and "Electronic Notarization" mean an official act by an electronic notary public that involves electronic documents.

(4)   "Electronic Notary Public" and "Electronic Notary" mean a notary public who has registered with the Secretary the capability of performing electronic notarial acts in conformance with this Article.

(5)   "Electronic Notary Seal" and "Electronic Seal" mean information within a notarized electronic document that includes the notary's name, jurisdiction, and commission expiration date, and generally corresponds to data in notary seals used on paper documents.

(6)   "Electronic Signatures" means an electronic symbol or process attached to or logically associated with an electronic document and executed or adopted by a person with the intent to sign the document.

(7)   "Notary's Electronic Signature" means those forms of electronic signature which have been approved by the Secretary as authorized in G.S. 10B-125, as an acceptable means for an electronic notary to affix the notary's official signature to an electronic record that is being notarized.

§ 10B-102. Scope of this Article.

Article 1 of this Chapter applies to all acts authorized under this Article unless the provisions of Article 1 directly conflict with the provisions of this Article, in which case provisions of Article 2 shall control.

Part 2. Registration.

§ 10B-105. Qualifications.

(a)   A person qualified for electronic notary registration shall meet all of the following requirements:

(1)   Hold a valid commission as a notary public in the State of North Carolina.

(2)   Except as otherwise provided, abide by all the provisions of Article 1 of this Chapter.

(3)   Satisfy the requirements of G.S. 10B-107.

(4)   Submit an electronic registration form containing no significant misstatement or omission of fact.

(b)   The Secretary may deny a registration as an electronic notary as authorized in G.S. 10B-5(d).

§ 10B-106. Registration with the Secretary of State.

(a)   Before performing notarial acts electronically, a notary shall register the capability to notarize electronically with the Secretary.

(b)   The term of registration as an electronic notary shall coincide with the term of the notary's commission under Article 1 of this Chapter.

(c) An electronic notary shall reregister the capability to notarize electronically at the same time the notary applies for recommissioning under the requirements of Article 1 of this Chapter.

(d) An electronic form shall be used by an electronic notary in registering with the Secretary and it shall include, at least all of the following:

   (1) The applicant's full legal name and the name to be used for commissioning, excluding nicknames.

   (2) The state and county of commissioning of the registrant.

   (3) The expiration date of the registrant's notary commission.

   (4) Proof of successful completion of the course of instruction on electronic notarization as required by this Article.

   (5) A description of the technology the registrant will use to create an electronic signature in performing official acts.

   (6) If the device used to create the registrant's electronic signature was issued or registered through a licensed certification authority, the name of that authority, the source of the license, the starting and expiration dates of the device's term of registration, and any revocations, annulments, or other premature terminations of any registered device of the registrant that was due to misuse or compromise of the device, with the date, cause, and nature of each termination explained in detail.

   (7) The e-mail address of the registrant.

   The information provided in a registration that relates to subsection (7) of this section shall be considered confidential information and shall not be subject to disclosure under Chapter 132 of the General Statutes, except as provided by rule.

(e) The electronic registration form for an electronic notary shall be transmitted electronically to the Secretary and shall include any decrypting instructions, codes, keys, or software that allow the registration to be read.

(f) Within 10 business days after the change of any registration information required of an electronic notary, the notary shall electronically transmit to the Secretary a notice of the change of information signed with the notary's official electronic signature.

§ 10B-107. Course of instruction.

(a) Before performing electronic notarial acts, a notary shall take a course of instruction of least three hours approved by the Secretary and pass an examination of this course, which shall be in addition to the educational requirements provided in Article 1 of this Chapter.

(b) The content of the course and the basis for the examination shall be notarial laws, procedures, technology, and ethics as they pertain to electronic notarization.

§ 10B-108. Fees for registration.

The fee payable to the Secretary for registering or reregistering as an electronic notary is fifty dollars ($50.00), which shall be in addition to the fee required in G.S. 10B-13. All funds received by the Secretary under this section shall be deposited into the General Fund.

Part 3. Electronic Notarial Acts, Powers, and Limitations.

§ 10B-115. Types of electronic notarial acts.
The following types of notarial acts may be performed electronically:
- (1) Acknowledgments;
- (2) Jurats;
- (3) Verifications or proofs; and
- (4) Oaths or affirmations.

§ 10B-116. Prohibitions.
An electronic notarization shall not be performed if the signer of the electronic document:
- (1) Is not in the presence of the electronic notary at the time of notarization; and
- (2) Is not personally known to the notary or identified by the evidence in accordance with other provisions of this Chapter; or
- (3) For any reason set forth in G.S. 10B-20.

§ 10B-117. Notarial components of electronic document.
In performing an electronic notarial act, all of the following components shall be attached to, or logically associated with, the electronic document by the electronic notary, all of which shall be immediately perceptible and reproducible in the electronic record to which the notary's electronic signature is attached:
- (1) The notary's name, state, and county of commissioning exactly as stated on the commission issued by the Secretary;
- (2) The words "Electronic Notary Public";
- (3) The words "State of North Carolina";
- (4) The expiration date of the commission;
- (5) The notary's electronic signature; and
- (6) The completed wording of one of the following notarial certificates:
  - a. Acknowledgment;
  - b. Jurat;
  - c. Verification or proof; or
  - d. Oath or affirmation.

§ 10B-118. Maximum fees.
For performing electronic notarial acts, the maximum fees that may be charged by an electronic notary are as follows:
- (1) For acknowledgments, $10.00 per signature.
- (2) For jurats, $10.00 per signature.
- (3) For verifications or proofs, $10.00 per signature.
- (4) For oaths or affirmations, $10.00 per signature.

Part 4. Electronic Notary Records, Maintenance, and Disposition.

§ 10B-125. Electronic signature, electronic seal.
- (a) The notary's electronic signature in combination with the electronic notary seal shall be used only for the purpose of performing electronic notarial acts.
- (b) The Secretary shall adopt rules necessary to establish standards, procedures, practices, forms, and records relating to a notary's electronic signature and

electronic seal. The notary's electronic seal and electronic signature shall conform to any standards adopted by the Secretary.

§ 10B-126. Security measures.

(a) A notary shall safeguard the notary's electronic signature, the notary's electronic seal, and all other notarial records. Notarial records shall be maintained by the notary, and the notary shall not surrender or destroy the records except as required by a court order or as allowed under rules adopted by the Secretary.

(b) When not in use, the notary shall keep the notary's electronic signature, electronic seal, and all other notarial records secure, under the exclusive control of the notary, and shall not allow them to be used by any other notary or any other person.

(c) A notary shall do the following within 10 days of discovering that the notary's electronic seal or electronic signature has been stolen, lost, damaged, or otherwise rendered incapable of affixing a legible image:

    (1) Inform the appropriate law enforcement agency in the case of theft or vandalism.

    (2) Notify the appropriate register of deeds and the Secretary in writing and signed in the official name in which he or she was commissioned.

(d) The Secretary may adopt rules necessary to ensure the integrity, security, and authenticity of electronic notarizations.

(e) The Secretary may require an electronic notary to create and to maintain a record, journal, or entry of each electronic notarial act. The rule-making authority contained in this subsection shall become effective 18 months after December 1, 2005.

(f) The failure of an electronic notary to produce within 10 days of the Department's request any record required by a rule adopted under this section shall result in the suspension of the electronic notary's power to act as a notary under the provision of this Chapter until the Secretary reinstates the notary's commission.

(g) Upon resignation, revocation, or expiration of an electronic notary commission, or death of the notary, all notarial records required by statute or rule shall be delivered to the Secretary.

§ 10B-127. Maintenance of electronic device.

(a) An electronic notary shall take reasonable steps to ensure that any registered device used to create the notary's electronic signature is current and has not been revoked or terminated by its issuing or registering authority.

(b) If the registration of the device used to create electronic signatures either expires or is changed during the electronic notary's term of office, the notary shall cease performing electronic notarizations until:

    (1) A new device is duly issued or registered to the notary; and

    (2) An electronically signed notice is sent to the Secretary that shall include the starting and expiration dates of any new registration term and any other new information at variance with information in the most recently executed electronic registration form.

§ 10B-128. Disposition of records.

(a) Upon compliance with G.S. 10B-127 and except as provided in subsection (b) of this section, when an electronic notary's commission expires or is resigned or revoked, or when an electronic notary dies, the notary or the notary's duly authorized representative shall erase, delete, or destroy the coding, disk, certificate, card, software, file, or program that enables electronic affixation of the notary's official electronic signature.

(b) A former electronic notary whose previous commission or application was not revoked or denied by the Secretary need not erase, delete, or destroy the coding, disk, certificate, card, software, file, or program enabling electronic affixation of the official electronic signature if he or she is recommissioned and reregistered as an electronic notary using the same electronic signature within three months after commission expiration.

Part 5. Certificate Forms.

§ 10B-135. Validity of notarial certificates.

The provisions contained in Article 1, Part 6, of this Chapter, with regard to notarial certificate forms, are applicable for the purposes of this Article.

§ 10B-136. Form of evidence of authority of electronic notarial act.

Electronic evidence of the authenticity of the official electronic signature and electronic seal of an electronic notary of this State, if required, shall be attached to, or logically associated with, a notarized electronic document transmitted to another state or nation and shall be in the form of an electronic certificate of authority signed by the Secretary in conformance with any current and pertinent international treaties, agreements, and conventions subscribed to by the government of the United States.

§ 10B-137. Certificate of authority for electronic notarial act.

(a) An electronic certificate of authority evidencing the authenticity of the official electronic signature and electronic seal of an electronic notary of this State shall contain substantially the following words:

Certificate of Authority for an Electronic Notarial Act

I, _____ (name, title, jurisdiction of commissioning official) certify that _____ (name of electronic notary), the person named as an electronic notary public in the attached or associated document, was indeed registered as an electronic notary public for the State of North Carolina and authorized to act as such at the time of the document's electronic notarization.

To verify this Certificate of Authority for an Electronic Notarial Act, I have included herewith my electronic signature this _____ day of _____, 20____.

(Electronic signature (and seal) of commissioning official)

(b) The Secretary may charge ten dollars ($10.00) for issuing an electronic certificate of authority.

Part 6. Enforcement.

§ 10B-145. Restriction or revocation of registration.
The Secretary or the Secretary's designee shall have the authority to warn, restrict, suspend, or revoke an electronic notary registration for a violation of this Chapter and on any ground for which electronic notary registration may be denied under this Chapter.

§ 10B-146. Wrongful manufacture, distribution, or possession of software or hardware.
(a) Any person who knowingly creates, manufactures, or distributes software for the purpose of allowing a person to act as an electronic notary without being commissioned and registered in accordance with this act shall be guilty of a Class G felony.

(b) Any person who wrongfully obtains, conceals, damages, or destroys the certificate, disk, coding, card, program, software, file, or hardware enabling an electronic notary to affix an official electronic signature is guilty of a Class I felony.

APPENDIX 2
FREQUENTLY ASKED QUESTIONS

General Information

1. How does a notary find information about statutory changes that affect notary practice?

Notaries can contact the Notary Section in the Department of the Secretary of State (919-807-2219), the county register of deeds office, or a local community college to learn about changes in the statutes that will affect notaries public. They can also consult the Department's Web site at www.sosnc.com or Chapter 10B of the North Carolina General Statutes.

2. What is a notarial act?

As defined in the statutes, a notarial act is any act that a notary public of North Carolina is authorized to perform, including:

- Taking an acknowledgment
- Administering an oath or affirmation
- Taking a verification upon oath or affirmation
- Witnessing or attesting a signature

Powers and Limitations

3. What are the notarial acts a North Carolina notary public is authorized to perform?

North Carolina notaries are authorized to perform acknowledgments, oaths and affirmations, and verifications and proofs.

4. If a notary resides in one county, can he or she notarize a document in another county?

Yes. A North Carolina notary public may notarize documents in any North Carolina county.

5. May a notary certify a true copy of a document?

No, a notary is not authorized to certify any document to be a true copy.

6. What is the difference between a "jurat" and an "acknowledgment"? Are the terms interchangeable?

No, the terms are not interchangeable.

- A *jurat* is that part of a notarial certificate in which the notary states that an oath or affirmation was administered.

- An *acknowledgment* is a declaration by a person that he or she executed an instrument for the purposes stated therein. If the instrument is executed in a representative or fiduciary capacity, the acknowledgment is also a declaration that the instrument was signed with the proper authority and executed as the act of the party represented and identified therein.

7. What is the penalty for notarizing a document without the personal appearance of the principal?

In addition to losing the notarial commission, a notary who performs a notarial act without the principal personally appearing before the notary is guilty of a Class 1 misdemeanor. If the notary performs the notarial act without the principal's personal appearance with the intent to commit fraud, the notary is guilty of a Class I felony.

8. What other notary act violations are classified as Class 1 misdemeanors?

- Performing a notarial act after a commission has expired or been suspended
- Performing a notarial act before taking the oath of office
- Taking a verification or proof without the subscribing witness personally appearing before the notary
- Taking a verification or proof of a subscribing witness without personal knowledge or satisfactory evidence of the subscribing witness's identity
- Holding oneself out to the public as a notary without being commissioned

9. What violations are classified as felonies?

- Performing a notarial act knowing it to be false or fraudulent
- Taking a verification or proof of a subscribing witness without personal knowledge or satisfactory evidence of the subscribing witness's identity with the intent to commit fraud
- Performing notarial acts knowing he or she is not commissioned under state law
- Knowingly creating or distributing software to allow an unauthorized person to act as an electronic notary
- Wrongfully obtaining, concealing, damaging, or destroying electronic notary technology
- Obtaining, using, concealing, defacing, or destroying a notarial seal or notarial records without the proper authority

10. Can an applicant who has been convicted of a felony become a notary?

According to G.S. 10B-5(d)(2), the Department may deny an application for commission or recommission based on "[t]he applicant's conviction or plea of admission or nolo contendere to a felony or any crime involving dishonesty or moral turpitude. In no case may a commission be issued to an applicant within 10 years after release from prison, probation, or parole, whichever is later."

11. If a commissioned notary is convicted of a felony or other crime involving dishonesty or moral turpitude, what should the notary do?

The notary should immediately stop acting as a notary and notify the Department. In most instances the notary will be given the option to resign his or her commission in lieu of revocation.

12. In what capacity may military personnel act as North Carolina notaries?

Persons authorized to act as notaries by 10 U.S.C. § 1044a and other federal laws may perform notarial acts only for certain categories of military personnel listed in those statutes. In doing so they are not acting as North Carolina notaries because their authority is derived from federal rather than state law. They may apply for a North Carolina notary commission if they wish.

13. If a notary notarizes a document, may he or she also act as a witness to that document?

No.

14. How does a notary properly notarize a document for a person the notary does not personally know and who lacks the customary proper identification?

A credible person the notary knows can verify the signer's identity.

15. May a notary take an acknowledgment by phone or fax?

No. According to G.S. 10B-3(1), an *acknowledgment* is a notarial act in which an individual

- at a single time and place *appears in person before the notary* and presents a record,
- is personally known to the notary or identified by the notary through satisfactory evidence, and
- either signs the record while being personally observed by the notary or indicates to the notary that the signature on the record is the individual's.

16. May a notary acknowledge two signatures if only one of the signers is present?

No.

17. What is the procedure for notarizing the signature of a person who cannot write but who signs with a mark?

A mark can be considered a signature in North Carolina, and the procedure is the same as for any other personal appearance associated with a notarial act. The notary would include the following language under the signer's signature (mark): "Mark affixed by *(name of signer by mark)* in presence of undersigned notary."

18. May a notary public notarize a document that is in a foreign language?

Yes, but the notarial certificate must be in English. G.S. Chapter 66 requires an English translation of the document for authentication.

19. How is a notary's signature authenticated on a document in this country?

Information on authentications may be found on the Department's Web site at www.sosnc.com.

20. How is a notarized document authenticated for use overseas?

Information on authentications may be found on the Department's Web site at www.sosnc.com.

Commissions

21. Is a notary applicant who took a course of less than six hours and who submitted an application after December 1, 2005, required to retake the course?

Yes. All applicants for initial appointment as a notary public who are not North Carolina attorneys who submit an application postmarked on or after December 1, 2005, must take a course of not less than six hours within three months prior to filing the application.

22. What are the testing requirements for initial appointment applicants?

A non-attorney applicant for initial commissioning as a notary public must pass an examination (scoring 80% or higher) at the conclusion of the six-hour course. The test will be administered by the notary public instructor.

23. Will incomplete applications be denied?

Yes. All questions on the application should be answered completely. According to G.S. 10B-5(b)(8), a person shall "[s]ubmit an application containing no significant misstatement or omission of fact."

24. Can notaries use initials or nicknames in the official commission name?

The applicant must use his or her legal name for commissioning, which excludes nicknames. The following are acceptable forms for commission names:
- John A. Smith
- J. Allen Smith
- John Smith
- John Allen Smith

The notary's stamp or seal name and the notary's signature must match the notary's commission name.

25. Is the applicant information submitted to the Department considered confidential?

The following information required for a notary application is designated confidential by G.S. 10B-7(b):
- The applicant's date of birth
- The mailing and street address of the applicant's residence
- The telephone number of the applicant's residence
- The last four digits of the applicant's Social Security number
- The applicant's personal and business e-mail addresses

26. How long does it take the Department to process a notary application?

Three to four weeks, if the application is complete and correct.

27. What are the procedures after someone submits an application for appointment or reappointment as a notary public?

After the application is approved, the applicant will receive an oath notification letter. The applicant will then have 45 days from the commission effective date (stated on the oath notification letter) in which to go to his or her county register of deeds office to take the oaths of office for the notary public commission. Registers of deeds charge $10 for administering the oaths of office.

28. Are notary applicants required to be United States citizens?

No, but according to G.S. 10B-7(a)(8), the applicant must prove legal U.S. residency by providing "[a] declaration that the applicant is a citizen of the United States or proof of the applicant's legal residency in this country."

29. Are applicants for reappointment to the office of notary required to have an elected official's recommendation?

No.

30. How far in advance may a notary apply for reappointment?

No earlier than ten weeks before the commission expiration date.

31. How much is the fee for reappointment, and how may the fee be paid?

The nonrefundable fee for reappointment is $50. It may be paid by check or money order; cash will be accepted only if presented in person. The fee may also be paid online using Visa, MasterCard, or Automated Clearing House (ACH) debit accounts.

32. Are there testing requirements for notaries applying for reappointment?

Yes, unless the applicant is a North Carolina attorney or the applicant has been continually commissioned as a North Carolina notary since July 11, 1991, and has never been disciplined by the Department. Other notaries applying for reappointment are required to pass a notary public exam with a score of 80% or higher. Applicants for reappointment may take the exam online at the Department's Web site at www.sosnc.com. These applicants will have three chances in 30 days to pass the exam. Applicants who fail to pass the exam after three attempts must retake the notary public course.

33. Does the Department notify notaries when commissions must be renewed?

No. The notary is responsible for keeping track of his or her commission expiration date and applying for recommissioning no more than 10 weeks prior to that expiration date.

34. Must a notary be sworn in upon each reappointment to office?

Yes. A notary is sworn in every five years upon reappointment at the register of deeds office in the county of commission.

35. If a notary does not appear before the register of deeds to take the oaths of office within 45 days of the commission's effective date, what happens?

The register of deeds returns the commission to the Department, and the applicant must reapply for the commission, including paying a new $50 application fee.

36. Can a notary be commissioned in the county in which he or she works if the notary resides in another county in North Carolina?

No. A commission is issued in the county in which the notary works only when the applicant resides outside of North Carolina.

37. Are notaries required to have the latest edition of the *Notary Public Guidebook* to qualify for reappointment?

Yes. According to G.S. 10B-5(b)(7), a notary shall "[p]urchase and keep as a reference the most recent manual approved by the Secretary that describes the duties and authority of notaries public." The most current guidebook is this book, the 2006 tenth edition.

38. Where can the *Notary Public Guidebook for North Carolina* be purchased?
The current guidebook may be ordered by

- ordering online at www.sogpubs.unc.edu;
- writing the School of Government, UNC Chapel Hill, CB #3330, Knapp-Sanders Building, Chapel Hill, NC 27599-3330;
- e-mailing sales@sog.unc.edu;
- phoning 919-966-4119; or
- contacting a bookstore in your area or at a local community college.

39. What must a notary do if he or she changes his or her name?

- Submit a signed notice of change to the Department within 45 days of the change.
- After receiving an oath notification letter from the Department, obtain a new seal and return the old seal by certified mail, return receipt requested, to the Department.
- Take the oaths of office at the register of deeds in the county of commission within 45 days.

40. Can a notary notarize documents while he or she is waiting for the name change application to be processed? If so, how does the notary sign his or her name?
Yes, a notary can notarize documents during this time. The notary should sign as previously commissioned until he or she receives the oath notification letter from the Department. The notary should then abstain from performing any notarial act until the oath is taken at a register of deeds office in the county of commission and the notary obtains a new seal with the new name.

41. If a commission was originally issued under a nickname, is the notary required to change the commission to his or her legal name?
Yes, upon recommissioning. Effective December 1, 2005, G.S. Chapter 10B requires that a notary be commissioned in his or her legal name.

42. What should a notary do if he or she changes both his or her county of residence and name simultaneously during the term of the commission?

- Submit a new application and fee to the Department of the Secretary of State.
- Complete the online reappointment exam.
- After receiving an oath notification letter from the Department, obtain a new seal and return the old seal by certified mail, return receipt requested, to the Department.
- Take the oaths of office at the register of deeds in the county of commission within 45 days.

Official Seals

43. If a notary changes employment, should he or she leave the seal at the previous place of employment?
No. According to G.S. Chapter 10B, the notarial seal is required to be "the exclusive property of the notary." Even if a notary's employer purchases any tool related to the

notarial office, such as the stamp/seal or guidebook, or even if the employer pays the notary's application fee, the notary remains responsible and personally liable for all notarial acts he or she performs.

44. What precautions must a notary take to secure the stamp or seal?

G.S. Chapter 10B requires that stamps and seals be kept "in a secure location."

45. What are the components of the notarial seal?

- The notary's name exactly as commissioned
- The words "Notary Public"
- The county of commissioning, including the word "County" or the abbreviation "Co."
- The words "North Carolina" or the abbreviation "NC"

The seal may contain the notary's commission expiration date, but if it does the notary must get a new seal upon reappointment every five years with the new commission expiration date.

46. What are the size and shape requirements for the stamp or seal?

A seal for a notary whose current commission was issued on or after October 1, 2006, must be of the following dimensions:

- The seal may be either circular or rectangular in shape.
- A circular seal may not be less than 1½ inches nor more than 2 inches in diameter.
- A rectangular seal may not be more than 1 inch high or 2½ inches long.

47. What should a notary do with the seal or stamp upon resignation?

Within 45 days of resignation or termination of the commission, the notary must send the seal or stamp by certified mail, return receipt requested, to the Department for proper disposal.

48. What should a notary do if the seal is lost or stolen?

Within 10 days of discovering that the seal is lost or stolen, the notary must, in the case of theft or vandalism, inform the appropriate law enforcement agency (typically the sheriff's office). The notary must also notify in writing the register of deeds in the county of commission and the Department. The notary should also inform his or her employer of the loss or theft of a seal.

Certificates

49. Can a notary use a facsimile or stamp for his or her official signature?

No. A notary's official signature must be signed by hand in ink on the notarized document.

50. What is a "venue"?

A *venue* is the location, including the state and county, where the notarial act takes place. The venue is not necessarily the notary's county of commission.

51. Should a notary change the venue if it is printed with the wrong state or county?

Yes. The notary authenticates all notarial acts by, among other things, setting forth the venue. This implies that the venue is true and correct, so if a certification includes an incorrect venue, the notary should correct it. It is also recommended that the notary initial and date any corrections made in the certificate.

52. Are both the stamp and signature required for a notarial act?

Yes. A notary must also complete the certificate. The notary's signature and stamp by themselves do not constitute a complete notarization.

53. Is a notary responsible for adding a notarial certificate, if needed, to a document?

No. The document maker is responsible for providing the correct notarial certificate. G.S. Chapter 10B sets out the requirements for notarial certificates and provides examples of acceptable certificate forms. These forms can be found on the Department's Web site at www.sosnc.com.

54. What elements constitute a sufficient certificate that is not otherwise prescribed by a particular statute?

An acknowledgment not otherwise prescribed by law includes the following:
- The state and county in which the acknowledgment occurred
- The name of the principal who appeared in person before the notary
- A statement that the principal who appeared in person before the notary acknowledged that he or she signed the record
- The date of the acknowledgment
- The notary's signature
- The notary's official seal
- The notary's commission expiration date

A verification or proof not otherwise prescribed by law includes the following:
- The state and county in which the verification or proof occurred
- The name of the subscribing witness who appeared in person before the notary
- The name of the principal whose signature is to be verified or proven
- A statement that the subscribing witness certified to the notary under oath or by affirmation that the subscribing witness is not a party to or a beneficiary of the transaction, signed the record as a subscribing witness, and witnessed either the principal sign the record or acknowledge his or her signature on the record
- The date of the verification or proof
- The notary's signature
- The notary's official seal
- The notary's commission expiration date

55. Must a notary's seal or stamp and signature be placed on the same page?

Yes.

Motor Vehicle Titles

56. When notarizing a vehicle title, should the notary charge the fees set by G.S. Chapter 10B or those charged by the Division of Motor Vehicles (DMV)?

North Carolina notaries charge the fees set by G.S. Chapter 10B. Tag agents in DMV offices charge the fees set by G.S. 20-42, which states that the DMV has authority to administer oaths and certify copies of records.

57. When a notary is notarizing a vehicle title, are both the purchaser and seller required to be in the notary's presence?

Notaries should direct questions regarding vehicle titles to the DMV at 919-715-7000 or consult the DMV Web site at www.ncdot.org/DMV.

58. Is a notary responsible for the proper completion of an assignment or reassignment of a vehicle title when notarizing these documents?

The notary must ensure that the document is complete *above* the notarial certificate before performing a notarial act.

59. Is a notary responsible for putting a lien on a car?

No.

60. May a notary notarize an assignment or a reassignment of a vehicle title for his or her spouse?

Yes, if the notary is not a named party on the title or does not directly benefit from the transaction. The Department highly recommends, however, that notaries not perform notarial acts for relatives.

Fees

61. How much can a notary charge for a verification or proof, since the notary is both witnessing a signature and giving an oath?

According to G.S. 10B-31,"the maximum fees that may be charged by a notary for notarial acts are as follows":
- "For acknowledgments, jurats, verifications or proofs, five dollars ($5.00) per principal signature"
- "For oaths or affirmations without a signature, five dollars ($5.00) per person, except for an oath or affirmation administered to a credible witness to vouch for the identity of a principal or subscribing witness"

APPENDIX 3
ADDITIONAL RESOURCES FOR NOTARIES

The Web site for the Notary Public Section of the North Carolina Department of the Secretary of State contains reference material, forms, sample notary acknowledgments and proof certificates, highlights and tips, and answers to frequently asked questions. Its address is: www.secretary.state.nc.us/notary.

The following is a list of Web sites posted by other state authorities about notaries and notary law in their jurisdictions. These addresses were last verified on August 24, 2006.

Alabama	www.sos.state.al.us/notary/index.htm
Alaska	www.gov.state.ak.us/ltgov/notary/
Arizona	www.azsos.gov/business_services/notary/
Arkansas	www.sos.arkansas.gov/corp_ucc/corp_forms/forms/Notaryhandbook.pdf
California	www.ss.ca.gov/business/notary/notary.htm
Colorado	www.sos.state.co.us/pubs/bingo_raffles/main.htm
Connecticut	www.sots.ct.gov/LegislativeServices/NPForms.html
Delaware	www.state.de.us/sos/nphome.shtml
D.C.	www.os.dc.gov/os/site/default.asp
Florida	notaries.dos.state.fl.us/
Georgia	www.gsccca.org/filesandforms/notaryforms.asp
Hawaii	hawaii.gov/ag/notary
Idaho	www.idsos.state.id.us/notary/npindex.htm
Illinois	www.cyberdriveillinois.com/departments/index/notary/home.html
Indiana	www.in.gov/business/notary/
Iowa	www.sos.state.ia.us/notaries/notary_handbook.html
Kansas	www.kssos.org/business/business_notary.html
Kentucky	www.sos.ky.gov/adminservices/notaries/
Louisiana	www.sec.state.la.us/notary-pub/notary-index.htm
Maine	www.maine.gov/sos/cec/notary/index.html
Maryland	www.sos.state.md.us/Notary/Notary.htm
Massachusetts	www.sec.state.ma.us/pre/prenot/notidx.htm
Michigan	michigan.gov/sos
Minnesota	https://notary.sos.state.mn.us/
Mississippi	www.sos.state.ms.us/busserv/notaries/notaries.asp
Missouri	www.sos.mo.gov/business/commissions/
Montana	sos.mt.gov/Notary/index.asp
Nebraska	www.sos.state.ne.us/business/notary/
Nevada	sos.state.nv.us/notary/
New Hampshire	www.state.nh.us/sos/notary.htm
New Jersey	www.state.nj.us/treasury/revenue/dcr/geninfo/notarymanual.htm
New Mexico	www.sos.state.nm.us/Main/Operations/Notary-Open.htm

New York	www.dos.state.ny.us/lcns/notary1.htm
North Dakota	www.nd.gov/sos/notaryserv/
Ohio	www.sos.state.oh.us/sos/info/notaryCommission.aspx?Section=2
Oklahoma	www.sos.state.ok.us/notary/notary_welcome.htm
Oregon	www.sos.state.or.us/corporation/notary/index.htm
Pennsylvania	www.dos.state.pa.us/bcel/cwp/view.asp?a=1111&Q=441325&PM=1&bcelNav=|
Rhode Island	www.corps.state.ri.us/notaries/notaries.htm
South Carolina	www.scsos.com/notariesbc.htm
South Dakota	www.sdsos.gov/adminservices/notaries.shtm
Tennessee	tennessee.gov/sos/bus_svc/notary.htm
Texas	www.sos.state.tx.us/statdoc/index.shtml
Utah	notary.utah.gov
Vermont	vermont-archives.org/notary/index.htm
Virginia	www.commonwealth.virginia.gov/OfficialDocuments/Notary/notary.cfm
Washington	www.dol.wa.gov/unfc/notfront.htm
West Virginia	www.wvsos.com/notary/main.htm
Wisconsin	www.sos.state.wi.us/notary.htm

The following Web sites for notary organizations provide information regarding educational courses, reference material, and other matters potentially of interest to notaries:

North Carolina Notary Association	ncnotary.org
American Society of Notaries	notaries.org
National Notary Organization	www.nationalnotary.org

The following print resources may also have useful information for notaries. Readers should ensure that the information is up to date.

Farber, Charles N. *2004–2005 U.S. Notary Reference Manual: A Guide to Notarization.* National Notary Association. Updated periodically.

ID Checking Guide, U.S. & Canada. Updated annually. Available online at www.idcheckingguide.com/us.asp.

Closen, Michael L., Glen-Peter Ahlers, Robert M. Jarvis, Malcom L. Morris, and Nancy P. Spyke. *Notary Law & Practice: Cases & Materials.* National Notary Association, 1997.

INDEX

acknowledgments
: general requirements for certificate of, 4.1.1
: notary power to perform, 2.1
: required actions, 3.1
: *See also* certificates

advertisements, prohibition against by notary, 2.2.7

affidavits, 5.1.1. *See also* certificates

affirmation
: defined, 3.1
: performing, 3.6

apostille. *See* authentication

application to become notary
: declaration required, 1.3.4
: fee, 1.3.4
: form, obtaining, 1.3.4
: generally, 1.3.4
: public official's recommendation on, 1.3.4
: required information on, 1.3.4

attestation
: commission expiration date, 3.5.4
: generally, 3.5
: notary's official seal, 3.5.2
: notary's official signature, 3.5.1
: notary's typed or printed name, 3.5.3

authentication, 3.7

certificates
: acknowledgment, Notary Act form, individual in own behalf, 4.2.1.1
: acknowledgment, Notary Act form, representative capacity, 4.2.1.3
: acknowledgment, Notary Act form, two or more individuals for themselves, 4.2.1.2
: acknowledgment, Notary Act forms generally, 4.2.1
: acknowledgment, short-form powers of attorney, 4.6
: acknowledgment alternative, attesting corporate officer, real estate, 4.4.2
: acknowledgment alternative, corporate officer, 4.4.1
: acknowledgment alternative, corporate officer, personal property, 4.5.1
: acknowledgment alternative, one grantor or maker, real estate, 4.3.1
: acknowledgment alternative, two or more persons, real estate, 4.3.2
: acknowledgment by attorney-in-fact, 4.7
: acknowledgment form generally, 4.1.1